Imelda Whelehan is Principal Lecturer in English and Women's Studies at De Montfort University, Leicester, where she has taught for over ten years. In addition, she is a mother and a cultural critic, who lives many of the contradictions outlined in this book. She has an insatiable thirst for good quality feminist debate and has written and edited a number of books, including *Modern Feminist Thought* (1995), *Pulping Fictions* (1996), *Trash Aesthetics* (1997), *Sisterhoods* (1998), *Adaptations* (1999), *Alien Identities* (1999) and *Classics in Film and Fiction* (forthcoming).

Popular Culture
and the Future of
Feminism

OVER*LOADED*

Imelda Whelehan

First published by The Women's Press Ltd, 2000
A member of the Namara Group
34 Great Sutton Street, London EC1V 0LQ

Copyright © Imelda Whelehan 2000

The right of Imelda Whelehan to be identified as the author of this work has been asserted
by her in accordance with the Copyright, Designs and Patents Act 1988.

British Library Cataloguing-in-Publication Data
A catalogue record for this book is available from the British Library.

ISBN 0 7043 4617 6

Typeset in Bembo by FiSH Books
Printed and bound in Great Britain by C.P.D. (Wales) Ltd, Ebbw Vale

For David, Miriam and Laurence, with love.

Contents

Acknowledgements

This book would never have come into being were it not for Kirsty Dunseath's interest in the first place. My greatest debt of thanks is, therefore, to her for approaching me with her ideas, and for providing support, judicious nagging, and acute detailed editorial advice throughout the lengthy process from initial proposal to finished manuscript. Any remaining deficiencies are, of course, my responsibility.

Many friends and colleagues have offered help, provided articles or references or snippets of information that have directly or indirectly inspired me. There are too many to thank personally, but special mention should be given to Kathleen Bell (and her daughter, Ellen), Nick Carter, Philip Davies, Martin Halliwell, Lucy Powell, John Roberts, David Ryan, Mark Sandle and Sarah Younie. Esther Sonnet has always been a source of inspiration, as has Lucy Zanetti; Chitrita Chaudhuri provided the lotions and potions to keep me almost in one piece; Mandy Jarvis allowed me to ransack her magazine collection and Carol Edwards preserved my sanity by allowing me to borrow her laptop after I smashed mine at the eleventh hour. Glynis Clarke has provided hours of worry-free time by her special care of Miriam and Laurence. Judith Smith typed the index with precision at short notice. Students at De

Montfort University over the years have also played their part, wittingly or unwittingly, in the production of this book.

No one did more than David Sadler and I can never thank him enough for the care and support he gave freely and at every level. No one did more to distract me (successfully, all too often) than Miriam and Laurence...

Popular Culture
and the Future of
Feminism

OVER*LOADED*

Introduction

It is now more than 30 years since a second wave of feminist activism emerged in the United States and Europe, most publicly marked by a demonstration outside the Miss America contest in Atlantic City in 1968.[1] The 'freedom trash can' set up at this event and into which were thrown items of women's underwear (as well as shoes, false eyelashes and women's magazines) was meant to symbolise an end of enslavement to an artificial feminine ideal; historically, it has meant that 'women's libbers' would be associated with bra-burning for ever. Even though the flames were the creative addition of a reporter, the image has stuck as part of our mass misremembering of the origins of the modern women's movement, so that younger women will continue to associate bra-burning with going too far; with going beyond the limits of rational protest.[2]

The image of bra-burning is always used to trivialise the achievements of modern feminism; bras are associated with the sexualised female image and bralessness is portrayed as far from natural – a practice likely to make one unfashionably droopy in later life. The reporting of the Miss America event used the 'sexiness' of the image in order to contain the 'danger' of the women's protest against competitive standards of femininity:

'Women who threw their bras away may have said they were challenging sexism, but the media, with a wink, hinted that these women's motives were not at all political but rather personal: to be trendy, and to attract men.'[3]

In the sixties and seventies, bras, underwear and bikinis were associated with saucy postcard naughtiness in British comedy – most notably in *Carry on Camping* (1969) – and the pert breast best connoted the 'girlie' or dollybird who never quite reached maturity. In the seventies and early eighties, bra adverts were one of the images of women attacked and defaced by radical feminists – particularly the Loveable brand, where the slogan 'Underneath they're all loveable' had the last word replaced by 'angry'. In the nineties, bra advertising experienced a renaissance, with model Eva Herzigova becoming the Wonderbra 'girl' in the 1994 Playtex campaign. The shoutlines, such as 'Or are you just pleased to see me?', deliberately underlined the purpose of the pneumatic push-up bra as having little to do with comfort or convenience and much to do with sexual attraction. The tribute to Mae West suggested a sassiness and playfulness which was never delivered.[4] In the newest round of 'bra wars', Pretty Polly's TV advertising campaign has stepped into the mêlée with bras made of the softest most 'natural' fabric supporting the most unnatural cleavage.

Breasts and bras, whether we like it or not, have dogged the women's movement since the sixties just as breast imagery has invaded the mass media and advertising until we appear to have reached saturation point. As Germaine Greer observes in *The Whole Woman*, breast awareness does not guarantee breast health,[5] and as long as men still focus on the breast as plaything and chief erotic curiosity, women will continue to have a faintly bewildered relationship to their breasts and, as a result, their body as a whole. Gone are the days when bras appeared to be marketed as a quasi-medical support to 'lift and separate'; now the emphasis is on the bra as a fashion accessory which creates a 'normal' breast profile that would otherwise be physically impossible to achieve. It appears that only the pneumatically uplifted breast is an object fit to be looked at, whereas the glimpse of a naked breast underlines how uncomfortable we remain with the 'naturalness' of nudity, as well as showing how far removed we are from the contours of the real female form. Naked breasts proliferate in tabloid newspapers, lad mags and soft porn, yet the breast of, for example, a prince's consort can unleash the wrath of a nation, seen as it is to symbolically compromise her virtue.[6]

The presentation of such 'heaving bosoms' is supposedly ironised so that we may bristle at the image but find ourselves disempowered in our attempts to find an adequate response, since the advert already 'knows' that it is offensive, to the extent that we are supposed to find it humorous and playful or be accused of not knowing the 'joke'. But what if the joke is on feminism and by extension women as a whole? And why, as Katharine Viner observes, is it 'always men who make the jokes, and . . . women who lose out by them'?[7]

Bearing this paradox in mind, this book offers a closer look at the cultural experiences of women in contemporary Britain, and the fate of feminist questions in a society where images of women as objects of desire proliferate and yet conflict with popular accounts of a world riven by a 'genderquake',[8] in which women can finally realise their true potential. In today's cultural climate feminism is at one and the same time credited with furthering women's independence and dismissed as irrelevant to a new generation of women who no longer need to be liberated from the shackles of patriarchy because they have already 'arrived'. Some have described this staging point as 'post-feminism'; others, such as Natasha Walter, have incorporated aspects of this with an 'old' feminist perspective and christened it 'new feminism'. For me, a definable thread runs through the language of culture, politics and the mass media that is quite simply anti-feminist and anti-equality.

Anti-feminist arguments, contrary to popular belief, do not just affect self-defined feminists; they act as a powerful rejection of *all* women's autonomy.

Yet at the beginning of the new millennium, feminists have been positioned as the cultural oppressors of 'normal' women against which a younger generation of 'new' feminists offers as antidote a marked individualistic kind of 'radicalism'. This radicalism pretends the power of self-definition is all about being 'in control' and 'making choices', regardless, it seems, of who controls the 'choices' available. Being 'in control' became one of the catchwords of the nineties in the parlance of women's magazines, but control always seemed to be about the right to consume and display oneself to best effect, not about empowerment in the worlds of work, politics or even the home. It was an expression of withdrawal from a wider political arena. In an increasingly 'global culture' there is little space for individual self-definition; our 'choices' have already been laid out, predicted and are being repeated by others simultaneously all over the world.

In 1992, the British publication of Susan Faludi's *Backlash* suggested that an ideological war was being waged against women to persuade them that female power is anathema to our health, happiness and above all our 'femininity'. Marilyn French's *The War Against Women* (1992) offered a similar point of view, casting patriarchy as tenacious, fluid and, like a particularly nasty virus, resistant to any attempts to eradicate it. Feminism, these two writers seem to argue, has produced the most vitriolic attack on women to date. A new anti-feminist swing attempts to recruit female apologists to confirm that feminism equals female tyranny and de-sexes women in the process; gender difference, it is argued, must be respected and it becomes more common to find populist science arguing that women are genetically disposed to perform certain tasks better than men – why these tasks always seem to include the menial, repetitive, domestic and caring aspect is a mystery yet to be solved.

The alleged 'genderquake' – the idea, popularised by Naomi Wolf, that the white male elite has lost its authority and is in the throes of losing its power[9] – has done little to change the attitudes of the majority of men to women, or between women from different classes, age groups, ethnicities or sexualities. Similarly, while the 'new' feminist has had a makeover and is presented to the world as youthful, stylish, relevant and accessible to both 'ordinary' men and women, she has yet to find her 'new' man. The 'new man' of eighties adland never became a fixture in the home and certainly never did the housework, but then it was never clear *what* he was for. For Wendy Dennis, 'He has to be gentle but not weak, malleable but not limp, masterful but not macho, sensitive but not sappy and stylish but not shallow. He has to cook! He has to clean! He has to garden and decorate.'[10] In short, he has to do everything, but he mustn't be effeminate or unsexily sensitive; it is therefore not surprising that the antidote to effeminacy, the new lad, emerged in his stead.

Self-centred, male-identified, leering and obsessed by sport, the new lad was naughty but nice; he proved himself a domestic catastrophe, but a certain boylike vulnerability supposedly made up for his deficiencies. Another slant on the new lad image is displayed in contemporary male confessional fiction, where new lad meets new man, and love of sport and other macho rituals are rationalised in more 'intellectual' forms. Either way, rather than endorsing a shift in male–female relations and the balances of power at work and home that currently exist, new laddism becomes a statement of intent; a series of common wisdoms about maleness and a firm assertion that there are psychological as well as physical explanations for the current cultural division of gender roles. Fundamentally sexist comments can be made under the shield of irony; if we complain, it is ample proof that feminists have no sense of humour. But from a feminist position it is difficult not to interpret the new lad as a nostalgic revival of old patriarchy; a direct challenge to feminism's call for social transformation by reaffirming – albeit 'ironically' – the unchanging nature of gender relations and sexual roles.

If finding a 'new man' in the outside world is generally a futile search, it is difficult to gauge the extent to which the new lad image has engendered, or is a reflection of, counterparts in 'real life'. The men's magazines such as *Loaded*, *Maxim*, and FHM where the new lad was refined, certainly attract a massive number of readers, but to assume that these readers internalise the lad credo in its entirety is to underestimate the uses to which popular culture is put by individual consumers. None the less, it is impossible to ignore the growth of this image and its depiction of masculinity. I suspect that its prevalence offers a timely warning to any woman who felt that gender relations were now freely negotiable.

The image of the new lad has filtered down from *Loaded* to TV sitcoms such as *Men Behaving Badly*, quiz programmes such as *They Think It's All Over* as well as nostalgia comedies which don't so much advertise their new laddish credentials as trumpet a 'golden age' free from political correctness. Examples of this nostalgic revival include ITV's *The Grimleys* or even *Goodnight Sweetheart*, where the 'hero' (Nicholas Lyndhurst) travels between the present day and the Second World War period, juggling the demands of his two wives. In this context any criticism of the portrayal of women is shielded by the excuse that this is a portrayal of the past rather than a commentary on the present; a portrayal which allows the stereotypical dollybird to get an airing (and to be internalised by another generation of young viewers) without any serious challenge from another female-oriented perspective. Chat shows are also infected with the new lad taint, most notably *The Frank Skinner Show*, where the eponymous host (bringing his new lad credentials from *Fantasy Football League*) enjoys a level of banter utterly reliant on the *double entendre*, and which at times depends on persistent flirtation accompanied by a level of questioning which assumes the interviewee is too dim to be concerned with anything but the most trivial.

The success of such programming, and its increase, suggests a ready acceptance of these images from some quarters of the audience. In addition, some of this material is both apposite and humorous – making it all the more difficult for viewers who experience pleasure in viewing, but are disturbed by less palatable undertones which suggest a celebration of female objectification.

Judgements on exploitation are notoriously difficult to negotiate; what is one to make, for example, of the feature on six female ballet dancers in underwear and rubber catsuits in the July 1999 issue of *Loaded?* Commentators have seen it as a piece of cynical media manipulation by the English National Ballet since such a photo shoot is bound to be picked up by the newspapers, and it is not a new notion to use sex to sell something altogether different. As is the case of all features in such magazines, our initial response is ambiguous: these are not anonymous females making a living from showing their bodies as pin-ups, yet the ballet's obvious celebration of the body becomes overtly sexualised in this context.

As many feminists have warned in recent years, sexism has become more complexly expressed, more sophisticated, and any response must demonstrate a similar degree of complexity. We are, after all, much more sophisticated viewers and consumers than we were a generation ago. Australian writer Catharine Lumby argues that 'far from representing the voice of patriarchal authority, the mass media is a daily reminder of the unstable ground on which notions of gender, sexuality and even nationhood are built in the late twentieth century.'[11] Clearly there are tensions in the way that messages can be received or appropriated, but the ground, though unstable, finds itself a firm enough platform for the perpetuation of a certain orthodoxy in the representation of gender or sexuality. In their approach to images, feminists, Lumby suggests, attempt to adopt a higher moral ground than the 'general public', who they accuse of acting in a bad faith to which they are immune. I think this constitutes a misreading of much influential feminist writing, in which I believe commentators are precisely trying to outline ways in which we are *all* dupes from time to time and how we *all* act in unconscious as well as conscious conformity to certain norms. Moreover, though we might all enjoy individual images or visual examples of 'political incorrectness', it is hard not to be aware that, in their totality, such images, utterances and perspectives show evidence of a renewed attack on contemporary female experiences. In 1929, Virginia Woolf felt moved to write that upon cursory examination of a popular newspaper, 'The most transient visitor to this planet... could not fail to be aware... that England is under the rule of a patriarchy.'[12] What, I wonder, would a latter-day martian make of our contemporary media?

If 'lads' have a female opposite I guess it has to be 'girls', with the Spice Girls as the fullest expression of contemporary girliness. Moreover, their promotion of 'girl power' suggests, along with Naomi Wolf and Natasha Walter, that today's woman is experiencing a genderquake in which there are infinite new opportunities. But what do girls really have the power to do? The Spice Girls represent an intervention into the male world of popular music, and they have unquestionably influenced thousands of young women by their promotion of the ideals of attainable success, independence and female friendship. Yet their credentials as models of female empowerment are distinctly dubious and their pre-pubescent audience may well encounter more subtle obstacles to girl power by the time puberty sets in.

The 'girlies' as represented by *The Girlie Show* represent another slant to the Spice Girl phenomenon which on the face of it emphasises the bonds that exist between women and the radical possibilities of a woman-centred subculture. In the process we are presented with women being 'themselves' – indecorous, raucous, aggressive and assertive with men – borrowing some of what have always been considered as the worst of male attributes. The 'ladette' knows what she wants and how to get it; vulgarity and sexual objectification of men is supposed to pass for sexual self-determination. There are knowing lampoons of traditional feminine concerns – such as dieting, personal adornment, pleasing men – but little to suggest that we've moved very far from the male gaze, not least since the girlie phenomenon on TV is strictly overseen by male producers. Ladettes in this forum engage in the kind of pointless male-bashing that would get feminists barred from the air.

The ladette offers the most shallow model of gender equality; it suggests that women could or should adopt the most anti-social and pointless of 'male' behaviour as a sign of empowerment. The Wonderbra, unsurprisingly, remains the essential style statement for a wannabe ladette.

Terms such as 'babe' and 'girlie' have commonly been used as a means of infantilising women and one of feminism's aims was to look carefully at linguistic uses of such terms – dismissed by critics, of course, as trivial nit-picking or as prudish political correctness. The 'lad', conversely, came of age in the nineties: from an epithet used to describe behaviour associated with adolescence, such adolescent behaviour has come to determine men's natural state of being, and women are implicitly asked to accept it, laugh along with it or reject it at their peril. If the only response available to women is to dub themselves 'ladettes' and join in the fun, the future for feminism and female empowerment looks bleak.

In some respects, however, it is astonishing that 'feminist' is still an epithet used easily by many contemporary women, including the Spice Girls, who offer by the term a model of empowerment which is intermixed with a clear grasp of the values of femininity of a most traditional kind. As Emma Bunton of the Spice Girls asserts, 'Of course I'm a feminist. But I could never burn my Wonderbra. I'm nothing without it!'[13] A new generation's engagement with feminism may throw up some surprising results in the next century, but this book is partly about the cost of forgetting or misrepresenting the landmarks in feminism's past.

It is believed that the actual term 'new lad' is falling into relative disuse, but it is still a part of populist parlance, and the behaviours and beliefs it connotes have acted as a rejection of political correctness and a challenge to female power. Whether at the time of reading you recognise the phenomenon or whether a new buzzword has taken its place, I guarantee that some potent manifestation of a backlash against feminism – particularly its more overtly political forms – will be in evidence. This book not only sets out to expose the ways in which such formulations emerge by looking at popular culture today, but also attempts, by example, to demonstrate that there is still a need for feminist critique in a world where these popular manifestations of gender inequality either inform or partially reflect the world as it is. When cast in this light, no individual image is 'trivial'.

Despite the fact that the impetus of my critique requires the pitting of some feminists against others, I do not mean to suggest that there is only one true path to 'enlightenment' in the form of a strict feminist orthodoxy. It is one of the chief intentions of this book to show how reductive the accusation of totalitarianism lodged by some 'new' feminists can be. Feminism is a flawed philosophy; but what makes up for its failings is the fact that countless women comprise the sum of its parts. It would be useful in some ways to be able to exclude some feminists from the reckoning and denounce their work, but feminism – and British feminism more distinctly than US feminism – has no 'club' that you can be barred from: this is its strength and its weakness.

None the less, you will be left in no doubt about which figures and which propositions I believe to be misleading or erroneous. For example, although I am not in complete disagreement with all its observations, I believe the dangers of so-called 'new feminism' are that it too casually claims that clear victories have been won and that the way forward is in the form of lifestyle choices and self-definition. It also too glibly presents 'old feminism' as having signally failed to speak to the majority of women, and in doing so misrepresents its scope, its political energy and its ability to learn from mistakes, as well as suggesting that the purview of 'new' feminism is much more inclusive than it actually is. I hope that, at the very least, readers will find in my critique a view of feminism as accessible, relevant and a useful means to imagine new futures and relationships between the sexes.

It is my belief that we have passed into an era of 'retro-sexism' – nostalgia for a lost, uncomplicated past peopled by 'real' women and humorous cheeky chappies, where the battle of the sexes is most fondly remembered as being played out as if in a situation comedy such as *Man About the House* or *Butterflies* (the latter repeated on BBC2 as recently as 1999). Such retrospective envisioning offers a dialogue between the past and the present and is symptomatic of a real fear about a future where male hegemony might be more comprehensively and effectively attacked than has so far been the case.

Representations of women, from the banal to the downright offensive, have a way of replicating themselves across the decades as if they tell us some fundamental 'truths' about femininity. What is most disturbing about this, as Myra Macdonald points out, 'is their tenaciousness, or the alacrity with which they have been defensively reinvented, against the cultural and social changes in women's lives'.[14] Contemporary 'truths' about sex and gender are being supported by the kind of populist scientific discourse that people find at once compelling and reassuring. Because science for many connotes the transmission of incontrovertible 'fact', any new 'findings' that argue that women and men are genetically programmed to behave differently are embraced cheerfully by a mass media always looking for a new angle on the 'battle of the sexes'.

For men and women, anxious about their identity at the dawn of the new millennium, the recasting of gender polarities in pseudo-Darwinian terms may be a suitable antidote. But it is important to recognise that research of this kind is always spookily 'timely', a reactionary response which unites with wider fears about the net effects of shifting social trends. If we take an example of research specifically about women in the workplace we can see how such findings have numerous applications. The *Sunday Times* in 1997 reported on findings that women were more frequently losing their hair 'because of "testosterone overload" caused by taking on traditional male roles in the workplace'. As the article progressed it suggested that a) women were behaving like men in the workplace in a will to succeed; b) this involved working twice as hard as men and c) it also involved juggling professional and domestic responsibilities in an endeavour to be 'superwoman'. Here we can see that the initial contention that women are paying the price of trying to be 'like men' is undermined by further evidence that they are actually being very much 'like women' – doing twice the work of their male counterparts for the same results and still taking chief responsibility for all domestic arrangements.[15]

The following chapters reflect on various cultural moments in an attempt to offer in miniature an anatomy of the backlash against feminism in Britain and by extension – because images and reflections transcend national boundaries – globally. In the process I hope to show that although feminism has been recently parodied and misrepresented as a prudish, authoritarian orthodoxy, its relevance has never been more obvious in the face of concerted attacks against female autonomy in general. As I have already hinted, some 'brands' of feminism are more appealing to me than others; I lament, for example, the descent of some of the most cogent and sparky elements of recent feminist critique into the rhetoric of 'lifestyle' choices and consumption and would want to assert that feminism carries with it social responsibility and ethical commitment. There is much that needs to be re-evaluated in any assessment of second-wave feminism's contribution to contemporary social and political life, but I believe it would be misguided to cast off some of this century's most important thinkers in an endless quest for new trends, new thoughts and new faces. Feminism's second wave created what we now think of as gender politics; previous incarnations of feminism wanted a piece of the action within the hallowed male establishments of politics, education and commerce, but the second wave wanted liberation from a civilisation seen to be shaped to accommodate men's needs.

Simone de Beauvoir articulated the experience of being a woman as being 'Other', outside and marginal, yet the female also defines maleness by being situated as its binary opposite: 'no biological, psychological, or economic fate determines the figure that the human female presents in society; it is civilisation as a whole that produces this creature, intermediate between male and eunuch, which is described as feminine.'[16] De Beauvoir's influence on modern feminists can be clearly seen in works such as Germaine Greer's *The Female Eunuch* (1970). In *The Whole Woman* (1999), Greer laments the all-too-hasty transition from calls to liberation to the language of equality, and succinctly outlines the difference: 'Seekers after equality clamoured to be admitted to smoke-filled male haunts. Liberationists sought the world over for clues to what women's lives could be like if they were free to define their own values, order their own priorities and decide their own fate.'[17] Before the smoke gets in our eyes it's time to look back at feminism again and determine what links the new and old and where the new will take us.

For feminists like me the juxtaposition between old 'seventies' feminism and new feminism leaves a yawning chasm that counts for my own experiences. Too old to be a 'new' feminist, and yet too young to have 'been there', I vaguely remember as a ten-year-old watching the muffled disturbances as British feminists disrupted the 1970s Miss World competition on television. It took me many years to make sense of it all, but out of this developed a growing conviction that feminism was relevant to the lives of women and men today and could offer bright, original, humorous and transformative perspectives on the patterns of gender relations at the turn of the century. It may, as Greer says, be time to get angry again;[18] and it certainly isn't time to be complacent.

Chapter One
Retro-sexism and the F-word

The new lad and the ladette could only have emerged in an atmosphere hostile to feminism. To understand the burgeoning popularity of these retro-sexist images, it is important to look at how perceptions of feminism have shifted significantly since the 1970s.

Modern feminism developed in recognition that many issues close to women had no language with which to express them. From this perspective feminism was engagingly oppositional and challenging, enabling women to identify themselves as an oppressed group who, united, could gain the power to contest some of the most enduring preconceptions about femininity and female potential. The development of a politicised language of feminism allowed women to pursue equal representation in the world of work, to argue that housework *is* work, to demand more control over their reproductive health, to reject the objectification of women and the perpetuation of an impossible and undesirable feminine 'ideal', and much more. This not only helped feminism's agenda get a more public airing, it also prompted significant shifts in practice in the spheres of employment, the law and medicine to the point that feminists could feel that they were making a real difference to women's lives.

Yet somewhere along the line, feminism has become the 'f-word', perceived to be an empty dogma which brainwashed a whole generation of women into false consciousness of their relationship to power. Just as feminist arguments appeared to be gaining wider credence, the 'backlash' gathered force, capitalising on all the anxieties confronting a generation of women who hoped to wage gender war in a society where, fundamentally, gender roles remained hopelessly unreconstructed.

Women have clearly made inroads into some previously male-dominated spheres, but the spheres themselves have not changed their bias towards the male/masculine perspective and needs. Women who rose to the challenge to 'have it all' (to borrow the title of Helen Gurley Brown's bestseller, published in 1982) found themselves for the most part unfulfilled and utterly exhausted, mainly because the dynamics in the home had not changed significantly and partly because one of the predominant images of the woman who worked in the eighties was that of the 'superwoman'. Having it all, many discovered, was tantamount to having none of it. Feminism was casually blamed for creating this monstrous creature as if not being able to do everything 'proved' that women should have settled for their traditional lot in life. Feminism has made huge advances in giving women the language and the confidence to make demands in the spheres of education, work and to a lesser extent politics, but no one could convince men it was in their interest to take up their share of the housework and household organisation. Let's face it, it wasn't. Domestic chores remain unremunerated and firmly associated with femininity, along with nurturing and passivity.

The old male order could issue coded threats to women on the verge of self-definition with suggestions that feminism made you unattractive, unmarriageable and miserable and to a large extent these threats would work because that's often how women, overworked at home and in the office, felt. The so-called 'patriarchy' kept all the trump cards in the wake of feminist agitation – the political clout, money, the arguments of biology, the threat of harm and the right to determine what constitutes a reasonable argument. The backlash has profited from the fact that little has happened to transform the dominant perspectives on sexual difference, meaning that although one can shift one's self-perception it does not stop the fact that others can continue to view you as profoundly self-delusioned and interpret your successes and failures in entirely gendered terms.

As Susan Faludi cogently demonstrated in *Backlash* (1991), the successes of second-wave feminism were, twenty years on, being turned into crimes against woman. Women, suggests backlash rhetoric, have been forced to turn their backs on their natural biological imperatives by entering the public sphere of full-time work, politics and higher education in their droves. Their natural bent for childbirth and homemaking is being dangerously postponed or perverted into careerism, and inevitable burnout and depression are the result. The backlash argument, as Faludi describes it, runs thus:

> Women are unhappy precisely *because* they are free. Women are enslaved by their own liberation. They have grabbed at the gold ring of independence, only to miss the one ring that really matters. They have gained control of their fertility, only to destroy it . . . The women's movement, as we are told time and again, has proved women's own worst enemy.[1]

The oldest argument used against feminism – that equality is incompatible with femininity and more particularly with motherhood, and women who attempt to take on a man's world will be effectively desexed – has been gathering force since the latter half of the eighties, capitalising on women's perception of the contradictions in the new opportunities available since the rise of the women's movement.

The backlash works by reassuring people that the 'old' values hold sway because they are undeniably true. This circular logic provides comfort to many, trapped as they are in the economy and vicissitudes of the old order; needless to say, many people, having invested a lifetime of faith in them and having transferred those values to their children, would prefer things to remain broadly as they are. By aping men, feminists, it is implied, have proved repellent to them: unloved, unnurtured, women are finding themselves unwed, childless and burnt out by the rigours of attempting to keep up with men in 'their' domain.

The media has been declaring feminism finished for the past decade at least and popular images of independent women as psychotic or neurotic have proliferated since the late eighties – who can forget Glenn Close's portrayal of the bitter, twisted businesswoman Alex in *Fatal Attraction* (1987)? More recently she played Cruella de Vil in Disney's live action version of *One Hundred and One Dalmatians* (1996) to similar effect, suggesting that almost a decade more of the reality of the working woman had done nothing to mellow her representation. The fact that it is Cruella who asserts that 'more good women are lost to marriage than to war, famine, disease and disaster' again positions the career woman as unnatural and even demonic; and in this case her femininity is sent up by extravagant camp.[2] Other representations, for example in *Disclosure* (1994), are even more extreme. Demi Moore plays a boss who, when her advances are turned down by a colleague (Michael Douglas), accuses him of sexual harassment, suggesting that feminist empowerment has created new legislation open to systematic abuse by women and the resulting victimisation of innocent men.

It is suggested that feminism is the preserve of only the unstable, mannish, unattractive woman who has a naturally difficult relationship to her own femininity; such people only want to spoil 'normal' women's lives by making them uncomfortable about their 'natural' life choices. In this light feminism is clearly cast as doctrinaire; backlash rhetoric therefore encourages 'ordinary' women to lift the scales of feminist propaganda from their eyes and return to a celebration of their natural differences.

Yet at the same time that the media sounds the death knell on feminism, other commentators want to stress the extent to which feminists have seized power over the way we think, suggesting conversely that feminism is alive and well and successfully ruining our lives. Many of these commentators, such as Christine Hoff Sommers and Katie Roiphe, would term themselves 'feminists' while, in common with the right-wing thinker Allan Bloom, they charge feminists with becoming the new thought police. They maintain that feminists have initiated a wave of political correctness on American university campuses which has denuded high culture and devalued higher education by unseating old canons of learning in favour of 'tyrannical' feminist ones.[3] When feminists are not poisoning the minds of 'our' young women they are encouraging them, as Roiphe would have it, to cry rape the moment a sexual encounter goes wrong. These perspectives on the American campus are extended to embrace discussions of the impact of feminism throughout Western culture and in many cases feminism is demonised as misrepresenting social reality to innocent women everywhere. Feminist discourse is repeatedly likened to fascism or Stalinist communism, as if it is an actively hegemonic force which has subordinated or suppressed other clusters of ideas.

Yet the notion of feminist dominance (particularly in the academy) is refuted strongly by other writers[4] because this myth allows feminist perspectives to be greeted with hostility or boredom and positions an opposing (usually male) view as the marginalised, oppressed and therefore 'weak' one. From my own experience of working in a university setting, it seems that even in this rarefied atmosphere feminist viewpoints are barely tolerated and are often regarded as simply a nuisance. In some universities the fate of women's studies (always embattled, often under-resourced) hangs in the balance. Feminism bores people these days to the point that the raising of certain problems – particularly questions about the representation of women – is cursorily dismissed as reactionary, or even anti-intellectual. Where previously feminist challenges might have been anticipated – even acted upon – it seems more common for a feminist perspective to be parodied, hostilely misrepresented or provocatively 'ignored'. This tactic has become all the more apparent in recent years, and feminist arguments are regularly dismissed as passé in a fashion which facilitates the elevation of what would once be known as anti-feminist arguments to the status of self-evident truths. Those who deal in backlash logic conveniently omit to acknowledge how important feminism has been to social progress and that feminist perspectives on rape, for example, have enabled important shifts in the legal system, police practices and the public perception of the crime.

The backlash coincides with a far sharper dispute about feminism's philosophical and political territory to the point where the question of the 'ownership' of feminism comes into view – best demonstrated by the title of Christine Sommers's book, *Who Stole Feminism?* (1994). There is the splitting of feminism into two major traditions, one which traces its lineage from suffrage movements in Britain and the US, where the radicalism of the second wave is an unfortunate hiccup, and one which sees feminism's second wave as necessarily and inevitably shifting the agenda from a question of rights within the existing political institutions to calls for liberation from such patriarchal establishments. Sommers and Roiphe are examples of adherents to the first tradition, seeing themselves on the whole, like Tony Blair, as 'non-ideological', where non-ideological connotes 'strictly liberal' and a denial of the existence of alternative perspectives. To claim to be 'non-ideological' is to appropriate the exclusive territory of 'common sense', which offers arguments as self-evident and even 'natural'; it is therefore perhaps no surprise that Blair's Minister for Women, Baroness Jay, is herself reluctant to use the term 'feminist', which has gathered more powerful and potentially revolutionary connotations.

Although Sommers and Roiphe are examples of feminist writers explicitly in the business of trashing what they see as feminism's more militant tendencies, and although there are a number of commentators only too willing to identify where feminism has gone wrong, the backlash is just as often the product of unconscious anti-feminism, or a consequence of the collision of quite disparate contexts where feminist ideas have been implicitly or explicitly called into question. In the latter case, the result is the suggestion of a 'cultural trend' which is then taken up by commentators as meaning the end of feminism. The danger of identifying cultural trends from such disparate data is that when it comes to gender politics, anyone can do it with little requirement for substantiation, and they often conveniently ignore all the other signs which show continuing interest and investment in modern feminism.

As Faludi asserts, 'The backlash is not a conspiracy, with a council dispatching agents from some central control room, nor are the people who serve its ends often aware of their role; some even consider themselves feminists.'[5] The backlash often comes from 'within' where 'reasonable' feminists (always liberal) set their (often elitist and individualist) agenda against feminist utopian visions of sisterhood and social/political communities. Second-wave feminists are accused of not addressing the needs of 'ordinary' women, and of blindly encouraging them to turn against their families and lovers by destroying the sanctity of their private lives in the wake of the slogan, 'the personal is political'. A new generation of feminists, unconsciously perhaps, returned to a sense of a 'natural' order of social/sexual relationships by attempting to measure the ways in which certain brands of feminism had 'gone too far'. If this is the logic of a new feminism, there can be no social or ideological change in structural terms, only cosmetic alterations: the only possible aim is equality within patriarchy, which indicates that for many women the possibility of imagining the transformation of society and gender relations (as well as race, sexuality and other oppressive divisions) is denied once and for all. It is as if many feminists got cold feet at the first sniff of revolution, and possibly explains the 'lifestyle' emphasis of new feminism, which implies that women can succeed by making fine adjustments to their identities and demanding similar ones at the level of equal opportunities policy.

Faludi's book in particular brought the notion of a backlash against feminism to a wider audience, facilitating broader debates about the mechanics of the backlash in different contexts. To extend her arguments and apply them to men's magazines and laddish television, the backlash is seen to function most effectively when concepts, interests and even the existence of second-wave feminism are suppressed altogether. History can then be rewritten with all evidence of gender politics evacuated and nostalgia for the old order can be celebrated unproblematically. As Ann Oakley observes: 'Backlash texts convince us in part because they discard the conceptual insights of 1960s and 1970s feminism. They return us to a world of naive understandings about the origin of social differences between men and women, which in turn permit naive conclusions about the nature and implications of some of the most significant social changes of the last thirty years.'[6] Many elements of popular culture display just such a longing for a world uncomplicated by female uppityness, where women perform the far simpler role of exciting fantasies and longings of a quite different order.

Political Correctness

From a traditionalist perspective, when it comes to evaluating the intellectual significance of recent feminist thought, the second wave invariably falls into the category of modish anti-intellectualism. Whatever register it adopts, feminism can't win. Where it engages with 'theory' it is accused of obscurantism; where it cultivates a mode of communication designed to be accessible it falls into the category of that which dumbs down the intellectual enterprise. The jargon sometimes used is one way of attacking feminism as exclusionary or elitist; the subject matter of some feminist enquiry provides plenty more ammunition for the sceptic. Either way, the raw material which feminists often have cause to scrutinise (Miss World, *Loaded*, sex tourism) does not always fall within the purview of that which is deemed suitable for philosophical, sociological, literary or scientific enquiry, further reinforcing a sense that feminists prefer to engage with debased forms of 'low' culture in a deliberate sabotage of the high ideals of intellectual life. Women have, of course, traditionally been positioned as avid consumers and producers of generic forms of culture such as the gothic novel, romantic formula writing, and soap operas and, to some extent, 'low culture' seems to embrace all these forms which come to be defined as feminine. It is therefore hardly surprising that women are adept at criticism and evaluation; still less surprising that feminists have developed responses to literature and the visual arts over and above the natural and social sciences in an environment where women who do enter higher education tend to congregate in humanities disciplines.

Feminism is a messy and repetitive business since it blurs intellectual boundaries and concerns itself with real lives as well as the ephemera of images and representation, and needs to be aware of cultural variance in its perception of how women are treated and represented all over the world. The tenacity of what I shall still call 'patriarchy' for short − the male-dominated masculinist agenda of politics, culture and environment throughout the whole world − requires that women who are feminists repeat the same fundamental demands about equality of opportunity, material equality, access to reproductive choices, freedom from violence and so forth. Yet, in the modern age, people are accustomed to things being renamed, rebranded, refashioned and given the prefix 'new' and are therefore bored and intolerant of repetition, which is associated with 'old' and outmoded (or unmodish) ideas. Others, perhaps sympathetic to feminist demands, are baffled to find that despite commonplace assertions that women's lot has improved immeasurably, many feminists are still busily claiming that things are no better or, in the case of Germaine Greer, asserting that things are worse: 'regardless of official ideologies our culture is therefore, by my judgement, less feminist that it was thirty years ago.'[7] For Greer, growing instances of mindless brutality such as road rage and the escalating images of violence celebrated in the media are a denial of freedom to anyone unable to compete on these terms, and a Hobbesian nightmare of a war of all against all.

Feminism from a backlash perspective is relegated to dogma, one of the last bastions of 'political correctness' which, along with pro-gay and anti-racist groupings, is regarded as attempting to gag the majority from exercising their rights to 'free speech'. Giving space to address the concerns of any of these groups is felt to be a usurpation of the rights of those who feel that their centrality in civilised society is being threatened. Political correctness is no longer recognised as a means to remove offence from our vocabulary and to recognise a broader range of experiences: at best it reminds people of otherness which is unsettling and at worst it inspires impatience and angry responses, sometimes including the testimony of a woman, black person, disabled person or gay person who agrees that it is all nonsense.

Political correctness as a term has taken on far less specific meanings, so that it is often summoned casually by people who feel that they are about to make a remark which contests a widely held belief, feel that they are simply being controversial, or wish to confront their listeners with an unpalatable 'truth'. Political incorrectness seems to offer individuals the chance to be naughty, to make a stand against the dreary old party line. In truth, of course, it has always been the politically correct who have been the mavericks, challenging the unthinking prejudices attached to the status quo.

Political incorrectness demonstrates an obsession only with the surfaces of things, just as 'lifestyle' fashions really homogenise rather than set you apart from the crowd. It legitimises the practice of superficial engagement with social realities and exempts one from the responsibility of engaging with less palatable ones, such as racism, poverty, sexism and environmental deterioration. The term has reached its nadir in the realms of popular culture where in relation to women it is used to connote a celebration of sexism, particularly a nostalgia for the portrayals of sexualised women typified by seventies comedy series such as *On the Buses*, where both 'clippies' and female passengers are easy prey for the lascivious and irrepressibly ugly Stan and Jack. This is nostalgia not for the 'real' seventies – nylon sheets, plastic shoes and all – but for the memories of the formative experience of viewing these portrayals and judging, perhaps, that they offered liberating linguistic 'freedoms' in their use of derogatory terms such as 'bird'.

This use of nostalgia seems to be confirmed by a newspaper advertising campaign for ITV's recent comedy series *The Grimleys*, which featured a head shot of the lead glamorous female character superimposed on an alphabet tutor card headed 'b is for bird'. The copy proclaims, 'a new politically incorrect comedy fresh from the 1970s'.[8] The series picks up on a current romance, among baby boomers especially, with all cultural artefacts of the seventies. But it also exploits its fictional setting to evacuate from the storyline any mention of feminism, firmly situating the woman featured in the advertisement as the chief object of sexual attention and promising a return to an older sexual economy. The humour depends upon a belief that people's relationships were more innocent in the seventies;

moreover, in effacing feminism, sexual tensions between men and women are played out along the lines of 'the traditional battle of the sexes', with feminine wiles pitted against masculine dissembling. Nothing, it is implied, least of all a few feminists, will change this kind of sparring.

The effects of other contemporary comedies such as *Men Behaving Badly* are more complex, since the male central characters, Gary and Tony, are set up as knowingly and assertively offensive and naively yet helplessly masculine respectively. In both cases they are rescued from complete obnoxiousness by their 'naughtiness' – this is thrown into relief by the indulgent irritation of the two female characters, Dorothy and Deborah – and by our psychological distance from them. Their characters and aspirations are on the whole kept distinctly two-dimensional so that empathy is difficult; instead they become the lexicon of bad male behaviour which viewers can identify in someone they know rather than themselves. The female characters have, interestingly, gone through much greater shifts as the series have progressed, until both, true to the backlash 'script', fall into line. Deborah moves from unemployment to becoming a student to suffering depression and lack of confidence to a relationship with Tony; Dorothy moves from a one-night stand with Tony to a relationship with a 'normal' man at work, to wedding plans and eventually a child with Gary.

Natasha Walter feels that the programme 'articulates the loss of masculinity, not its power, by giving us laddishness as a fragile pose',[9] yet this effect of fragility is also a plea for women to indulge masculine 'weaknesses' not necessarily because they are inevitable or right, but purely because they are so absurd. The humour of the predicament of these female characters – near the knuckle to say the least – lies in their gradual acceptance of their 'destinies' with Gary and Tony, who themselves by implication accept a certain repression of their worst 'masculine' traits. There is no doubt that the series is funny and multilayered: by identifying it as a 'lad' production bound up with backlash sentiments is not to detract from that. The task for feminism in the future is to feel able to focus on images and scenarios which are contradictory, as well as empowering others to identify elements of 'post-feminist' thinking with which they are uncomfortable. Feminism needs to find a better means to articulate this ambivalence about whether what is funny or apposite can also be offensive.

Victims and Victorians

The backlash, in common with 'new' feminist thinking more generally, also accuses feminists of encouraging a pathology of victimhood that makes them masochistic and reactionary in their perception of change. For Katie Roiphe,

> there are more than two sides to any issue, and feminists are closer to their backlash than they'd like to think. The image that emerges from feminist preoccupations with rape and sexual harassment is that of women as victims, offended by a professor's dirty joke, verbally pressured into sex by peers. This image of a delicate woman bears a striking resemblance to that fifties ideal my mother and the other women of her generation fought so hard to get away from.[10]

Roiphe assumes here that to take issue with verbal or physical harassment is to be weak or passive, an assumption which seems to me illogical and the result of scant attention to the majority of feminist arguments; it could be argued that to make the offence plain is to assume a position of strength and robustness. Of course her other point is that many of these incidents are too trivial to warrant any response, but without specific examples and their contexts it is impossible to adjudicate on this: suffice to say that the main point was to enable collective and public protest against the worst effects of female oppression. The point of establishing a language of victimhood, so to speak, was primarily a means to articulate the ways women suffer injustice, persecution or even abuse for situations which are not of their making. Feminists in the late sixties, in an attempt to galvanise a movement seeking transformation, wished to show how countless women's aspirations, talents and work were sacrificed to patriarchal imperatives, subjected at best, in Mary Ellmann's words, to 'an intellectual measuring of busts and hips'.[11] Only latterly has victimhood come to connote purely individual responses to slights or cruelty and therefore had its scope and importance somewhat diminished.

With the above remarks of Katie Roiphe in mind it is interesting to note that the present day, in Britain at least, seems to have generated a renaissance in the 'dirty joke' and also appears to be enjoying new ways to celebrate the sexual objectification of women – for instance, in the fairly new growth industry of lap dancing. Richard Thomas, pondering claims that more and more women are gaining high-status jobs in the professions, suspects that for every successful woman in the traditionally male professions, more women are attracted to the lucrative and burgeoning female professions of table and lap dancing: 'women's success in the workplace may be provoking a backlash among men who are looking for new ways to express their masculinity.'[12] In essence, he is arguing that the erosion of the sexual division of labour as demonstrated by the increased presence of women in the professions is counterpoised by a correlative growth of female labour in what might loosely be termed the sex industry. It is entirely possible, even probable, that an emerging shift in the demographics of work, with women often finding it easier to gain employment over their male peers (although not necessarily in permanent full-time work), is prompting some men to reaffirm their masculinity in the recreational objectification of women.

In *The New Victorians* (1996), subtitled 'A Young Woman's Challenge to the Old Feminist Order', Rene Denfeld argues, in common with Katie Roiphe, that second-wave feminism is making victims out of women; worse, she suggests that feminist critiques of sexual violence and power relationships within sex are akin to the arguments around chastity produced in the Victorian period. Here Denfeld offers a sustained critique of what has come more popularly to be seen as a puritanical streak in contemporary feminism. Denfeld's selection of feminists focuses primarily on those who many, in Britain at least, might see as unrepresentative of debates on sexuality, sexual violence and sexualised images – such as Andrea Dworkin, who is well known for her uncompromising stance on anti-pornography legislation.

In common with Roiphe, Denfeld paints a picture of American campuses dominated by feminist elders terrorising young women with overblown statistics about one in three women being vulnerable to sexual assault during their lives. For Denfeld, 'This is the danger of New Victorianism. This feminist promotion of repressive sexual morality and spiritual passivity promulgates the vision of an ideal woman, sexually pure and helpless yet somehow morally superior to men and all male-influenced institutions.'[13] In her view this amounts to a re-polarisation of men and women, 'men as wicked demons with sex on the brain, women as defenseless, chaste innocents in need of protection'.[14]

Many feminists, myself included,[15] have argued that some wings of radical feminism offer such an all-embracing model of patriarchy that they portray a sense of the inevitability of female oppression by supporting biologistic assumptions that men are more inherently aggressive and sexually acquisitive than women. It has also been demonstrated that debates about sexuality within feminist discourse have tended to focus more often on the negative patriarchal constructions of female sexuality and their oppressiveness to women, rather than on new and empowering definitions of desire freed from the spectre of the male gaze. Many of us would heartily agree with Lynne Segal that 'reclaiming sexual agency for heterosexual women can help revive a richer and more inspiring feminist culture and politics,'[16] but feel obliged to observe that we have not yet developed a new language of female (hetero)sexuality which deflects that used in contemporary erotica and women's glossies. It is clear that many women today, dissatisfied with perspectives which seem to tell them only what is wrong with female sexuality, rather than what is right, may choose to dub feminists old prudes and look to other accounts of modern sexuality which purport liberation from the repressed past.

In defence of feminism, one might aver that denouncing oppression seemed to be more pressing than pursuing new shapes of female desire that perhaps could not be realised in that climate. But this doesn't mean that in the late sixties and seventies radical feminists, while busily itemising the means by which sexual relationships oppressed women, weren't also trying to liberate women too. One has to try to envisage the type of sexual culture within which such women grew up – not too difficult if you consult the likes of Shere Hite's *The Hite Report: A Nationwide Study of Female Sexuality* (1977).[17]

Similarly Anne Koedt's 'The Myth of the Vaginal Orgasm' (1968),[18] read so often as a turning away from penetrative sex and a flirting with wholesale political lesbianism, perhaps more subtly tried to displace penetrative sex as the model of heterosexual union and enabled women 'to escape from male definitions of "normality" and "frigidity" to feel they had the right to make demands'.[19] An important if controversial text in its own right, it shows that there were attempts to imagine a world of sexual relationships freed from the taint of patriarchy, even though more often than not concerns with issues of the here and now took precedence. Needless to say, the politics of the personal were not always easy to translate into practice when they involved taking a long hard look at one's own desires and preferences. Feminists could be as reticent as any other group when it came to subjecting their own most deep-seated desires and motivations to 'political' scrutiny.

To equate second-wave feminism's views on sexuality with Victorian moral-purity campaigners denies the fact that much feminist work is clearly invested in the idea that sexual behaviour is for the most part socially learned and can be transformed. It would be equally appropriate to accuse producers of modern-day pornography and erotica of being 'new Victorians' in that they rely heavily on the 'hydraulic' model of male sexuality, depicting the male sexual response as a 'caged beast' which, once released, is impossible to control. The feminist position on porn, simplified by Denfeld to one which is pro-censorship and anti-pleasure, is seen as further confirmation of its Victorian repressive tendencies. Denfeld argues that 'by blaming sexual material for sexual violence, current feminists invoke the Victorian-era belief that sexuality is inherently evil and any display of it must be squashed'.[20]

This view of porn relies fundamentally on the work of Andrea Dworkin and Catharine Mackinnon and their activism and alliances with right-wing moral crusaders in the United States, attempting to pass ordinances banning pornography and asserting its links to crimes of sexual violence. In reality, feminist views on pornography are wide ranging and various. Many do wish to investigate possible links between the use of porn and violent crimes against women, without necessarily wanting to suggest that there is any simple relationship between such consumption and behaviour. Many recognise the dangers of inviting more repressive censorship codes for this issue (as they tend to bring more oppressive effects to the 'outsiders' and minorities first), yet remain concerned about the circulation of hard-core imagery. More still feel that the boundaries defining what is pornography are too restrictive, and that there is a need to address the representation of women in more general terms since 'softer' images (such as those found in *Loaded*) borrow conventions directly from porn and, arguably, tell us far more about the way the female body, and by extension femininity, is used in society today. Following on from this, some would prefer to deny porn its single-issue status by placing studies in relation to a wider consideration of how women are depicted and why. Feminists in general are very much aware of how censorship safeguards the establishment first and foremost, and yet for many the relationship of women to porn and porn to sexual freedom, or indeed sexuality of any kind, is an uncertain one.

Backlash rhetoric specialises in over-simplifying issues that have quite complex and wide-ranging implications in order to repeatedly make the banal point that feminists are just a nasty bunch of spoilsports. Feminists are broadly depicted as intolerant of criticism and anxious to ensure that the party line goes unsullied: 'using the cry of "backlash" whenever current feminist trends are criticised, New Victorians have effectively muzzled discussion within the movement – and, it would seem, outside the movement.'[21] I would argue that it is feminist critiques that are trapped within this account of their likely response to detractors; and this image of feminists as intolerant ideologues certainly holds sway in populist accounts of 'ordinary' women's views of feminism.

New (In)equalities?

Many younger women are impatient with what they see as feminism's obsessive attention to the images and effects which surround us, arguing that more energy should be directed towards the 'everyday' issues of education, equal pay and so forth. Denfeld is, if anything, a pragmatic feminist who wants action on the issues that most profoundly affect her. Liberal feminist in her leanings, she wants equality and simply wishes to ensure the policy processes are in place to see this through. Such women refuse to see any link between ideas and representations and things, but for me the link is inevitable, and this book is testimony to that belief. Any equal opportunities legislation is only effective if popular perspectives on the effects of one's gender on one's professional abilities also shift. There is no point in a female barrister, for example, obtaining equal pay and equal promotion if her hormones are blamed the first time she loses a case. This is also true of questions of race and disability, but the assumption seems to be that the 'young women' addressed are exclusively white and middle-class, and indeed this shapes the political agenda of the majority of new feminists.

As it is, too many women are aware that using the legal processes around equal opportunities may win you the case but lose you your career – whether 'new' feminists like it or not, women become the victims in this situation. Equal opportunities is a complex construction which at the present time cannot but reinforce the sense of huge inequality which operates in so many working environments. Also calls for equality don't do enough to recognise that structural inequalities between women ensure some a more privileged position than others.

To be fair to Denfeld, the other reason she alights on these issues is clearly an impatience to see things being done in the US other than the high profile anti-porn battles. Of course the issue of whether 'old' feminism speaks to a new generation is a live one; as Denfeld herself says, 'The same rights and freedoms feminists won for us have allowed us to develop into a very diverse generation of women and we value our individuality.'[22] Her idea that small groups, in preference to large feminist organisations, should take it upon themselves to champion specific feminist causes seems to me a recipe for further political atrophy and chaos, but would certainly win the approval of backlash propagandists who can see the virtues of divide and rule. In a sense, though, writers like Rene Denfeld are the key to the power of the backlash; they interpret all dissent among feminists as conflict and act as if the overall impact of second-wave thought has been malevolent.

Rosalind Coward, in her new book, *Sacred Cows* (1999), rejects the notion of backlash because she believes it polarises and over-simplifies debates around feminism to 'Are you for it or against it?'[23] Coward implies that changing social and political realities necessitate a new analysis of power where gender is a less crucial determining factor. For Coward, 'it is no longer a simple coherent picture of male advantage and female disadvantage',[24] and she feels that feminism will only continue to have relevance if it embraces the problems men face in a rapidly changing world. Coward is certainly profoundly sceptical about whether feminist analyses of inequality adequately reflect newly emerging social arrangements in which she sees gender as having less relevance in a more complex web of power relationships. Indeed, she argues that 'some of feminism's fundamental tenets aimed at redressing inequalities between men and women may now be adding to the widening gulfs between rich and poor, between unemployed and employed, between different communities'.[25]

For Coward, the eighties was the decade of the woman (signalled most predictably by the ascendance of Margaret Thatcher) and by its end 'men were in the eye of the storm.'[26] Certainly there is clear evidence that men as a group are suffering acutely from escalating changes in job security and employment practices, but how one might choose to approach this is a moot point. Coward's construction of this course of events inevitably positions women, or feminism more specifically, as in some sense to 'blame' for a shifting global economy. It is implied that events feminism set in motion have contributed to the economic disenfranchisement of men, but feminists might want to be wary of this backhanded tribute to their success if the conclusion shifts to an acceptance of the view that men are the victims now. Even if Coward doesn't go quite that far she does affirm that 'The old feminist equation that being a woman necessarily entails low income and low status is no longer always true, even if it sometimes is.'[27]

This is another troubling aspect of the backlash, where profound scepticism about the impact and gains of feminism comes dangerously close to rejection of any of its virtues or successes. Coward's writing goes some way to questioning the rectitude of her own feminist involvement over the years, as in her book women's rights dissolve into 'human rights'. In common with more vehement US critics, she suggests that there is feminist dogma and therefore the possibility of feminist heresy – the most obvious one from her point of view being that some women just want to stay at home with the kids and adjust their work accordingly if only feminism would let them.

I've never found a feminist 'bible' complete with commandments to this day, but if backlash truisms were ever to be believed, these commandments would run into thousands (if an entrepreneurial person were to create one, I feel certain there would be a demand – if only among feminist detractors!), and qualifying as an authentic feminist would be harder than becoming Pope. We don't need backlashers to tell us that feminism is riddled with loopholes and flaws, as well as being as slippery as an eel. Second-wave feminism was not born, with its rule book intact, out of the first beauty competition protests and women's liberation conference. It has developed in range and sophistication ever since, and during the past fifteen years or more 'rainbow' coalitions which allow for multiple perspectives on human oppression have become the norm. This is not to deny that the feminist 'mainstream' (that which gets most air time in either positive or negative terms) is still dominated by white, heterosexual, middle-class, youngish to middle-aged, able-bodied women; but this is more obviously true of the female contributors to the backlash.

Perhaps the most obvious feature of backlash rhetoric is its wish to personalise the political agendas of feminism. In an ironic reversal of this feminist stance, backlashers seek those issues which most closely affect their personal life or those of their peers and propagate a mood of anxiety if not to say moral panic around them. For Sommers and Denfeld it is the malign existence of women's studies programmes and radical groups and the way they 'confuse' the young about contemporary social/sexual relationships; for Coward it is anxiety about the future of the family, motherhood, and the need to offer positive male role models. Of these the one I have most sympathy for is Coward; feminists have often said that women's liberation will transform men's lives too, and I believe that is a commitment which needs renewed attention – but only alongside the commitment to fight until women's global equality is formally, materially and ideologically recognised.

Meanwhile, the backlash has an insidious power, most obviously because as Faludi suggests it can work on an unconscious level. It certainly undermines three decades of feminism by recasting its leading thinkers as necessarily conflictual, power-crazed and blind to the needs of the 'real' women – in doing so remodelling them along the lines of the lead figures in any major (male-defined) political party. Its influence is most clearly felt among those that have the most passing acquaintance with feminism, particularly a younger generation of men and women who feel that women have arrived, or even taken over. The rest of this book will discuss the effects of this 'unconscious' backlash against feminist ideas and attempt to identify those perspectives which, in the view of this author, make feminism as relevant today as it was thirty years ago.

Chapter Two
Girl Power?

Women have become quite accustomed to the epithets 'girl' and 'girlie': both remind us of our status as honorary children; both have in the past been used universally to position unmarried women – if you are not someone's wife, you are still your parents' girl. The term 'girl' also has cultural variations, so that in black African-American and African-Caribbean contexts it may have been more consistently used in a positive, sisterly fashion, yet the dominant meanings of this term currently in circulation are only superficially laudatory. Girls, made as they are of sugar and spice, suggest sweetness and a pleasing nature, yet there are other connotations (of 'girlie' in particular) which are more seedy, pertaining to sex magazines and explicit 'glamour' shots of women. The girl/girlie icons of today, in appropriating a term with such controversial provenance, cannot avoid echoes of its previous incarnations. None the less, the 'girlie' of today, at her best, notionally offers a subversion of the pin-up image: she is active rather than passive, and ruthlessly self-seeking in her own pleasures. Outspoken and sometimes aggressive, the new girl has no truck with feminine wiles, yet she looks deceptively like a pin-up.

The term 'girl power' will ultimately be remembered as the catchphrase of the Spice Girls, who burst on to the music scene in 1996. Their popularity, presentation and their evocation of 'power' provides a typically thorny problem for contemporary feminism. Girl bands offer a ground-breaking model of intervention into a male-dominated arena, yet girl bands, in common with boy bands such as Boyzone, are cynically written off as stage-managed and orchestrated by a shady Svengali figure looking for a profitable product to sell to the lucrative teen market. The Spice Girls, arguably unlike Boyzone, have managed to spin beyond the orbit of teen pop as newsworthy ambassadors of 'Cool Britannia' and as post-feminist icons up there with Madonna. These 'girls' are constantly quizzed about their attitudes to femininity, and their vision of 'girl power' plays on the illusion of a contemporary culture full of ready choices and opportunities for self-expression available equally to all women. Girl power adds fuel to the myth that young women are 'in control' of their lives and as such offers a more positive liberatory message to young women than contemporary feminism ever could.

Of course the Spice Girls were not the first female vocalists to be used as a model of resistance and a basis for aspirations. In the 1980s Madonna flouted the rules of conventional female behaviour with her overtly sexual style. Who can forget her Amazonian corsetry, the conical breasts an aggressive and ironic comment on male erotic obsession? Her 'Girlie Tour' in 1994 added impetus to the girlie 'movement' and certainly demonstrated the more transgressive potential of the figure of the girlie, inspiring Channel 4's commissioning editor David Stevenson to develop *The Girlie Show* in 1995.[1]

Equally, the Spice Girls are not the first all-female band to achieve widespread commercial success. Contemporary girl bands have many famous foremothers, ranging from The Supremes through to Bananarama. In the former case, the term 'girl' was used about them with assertive and unthinking sexism, in the way that 'girl' often refers to grown women in everyday speech. For Bananarama, coming to fame in the eighties, to claim to be an all-women band would have been regarded as making some kind of unattractive and humourless political point. Instead the group were cheerfully parodic – made-up and glamorous, but also quirky in a style that derived as much of its impact from adolescent fashion than anything else.

In the nineties the perils of claiming space as an all-women band were greater if you wanted to be popular, and the Spice Girls avoided any taint of political correctness by their positive embracing of the term 'girl', to the point where it became its own declaration of liberation and independence – a sassy refusal to be pushed around. Just as these all-women bands have found their chief fan-base among adolescent girls, so we may be forced to conclude that the most positive effect of the word 'girl' is that it summons up memories of choice and relative freedom before the travails of womanhood set in. This message has been the stuff of women's stories since *Little Women* (Alcott 1868) and perhaps before. Nor is 'girl power' new in the sense that young women in the sixties were memorising the lyrics and choreography of girl groups, both emulating the bands and using their lyrics to express their own teenage confusions. As Susan J. Douglas observed, 'While girl group music celebrated love, marriage, female masochism, and passivity, it also urged girls to make the first move, to rebel against their parents and middle-class conventions, and to dump boys who didn't treat them right.'[2]

In a more concrete demonstration of 'girl power', the Spice Girls did exactly that when they fired their Svengali, Simon Fuller. Yet life beyond their manager has not been smooth, with the departure of Geri Halliwell in the spring of 1998 and the vulturous press coverage of her initial disappearance, which was seen to show predictable cracks in the mould of girl power. Molly Dineen's documentary about, and commissioned by, Halliwell, screened on Channel 4 on 5 May 1999, depicts a simultaneously insecure but egocentric figure who is lonely and utterly dependent on fan adoration. Predictably, this rather sad representation was still used as a vehicle, consciously or not, to promote her first solo single, 'Look at Me', which was released days later. The trope of secret vulnerability is, of course, a celebrity staple and the triumph of the documentary is in not knowing how naive or how savvy Halliwell really is.

The 'celebrity self' as a role, a conscious performance, is compatible with the image of the Spice Girls in their *Girl Power!* (1997), which purports to enable the fan to 'find out exactly what us Spice Girls are really like; what we think, what we love, what we hate, how we live'.[3] *Girl Power!* capitalises on the identification of the Spice Girls as role models for teens and pre-teens, and is at pains to present them as normal 'girls' who like nothing better than a laugh with their mates.

Critics of the Spice Girls have had to acknowledge that to their teen audience they represent women achieving success on their own terms, regardless of the means by which they shot to stardom. Geri Halliwell's new role as United Nations Goodwill Ambassador has recently taken her to the Philippines as a pro-choice spokesperson for contraception, and what is made clear in Dineen's documentary is that she was selected precisely because of her high-profile impact on young women. Of course successful wealthy women have adopted the role of 'charitable benefactor' for centuries, it being one of the available and acceptable roles for women with a high public profile. But it is interesting to find a teen icon becoming associated with issues of fertility and its control – particularly since the UK has such a high rate of teenage pregnancy – although it is generally acknowledged that the mission is unlikely to realise its aims, given staunch religious opposition.[4] UK girldom takes on a potentially global feminist edge and while Geri Halliwell remains disarmingly frank about her own perceived limitations and ignorance about some of the issues (the documentary shows her nearly making the gaffe of asserting that she is pro-life in her preparation for her press conference), representatives of the United Nations make it clear that her fame is enough. This sets up a deeply problematic relationship between girl power and feminist issues where it is not Halliwell's feminist credentials that are in demand, but purely her stardom.

None the less, girl power marks a positive shift in the gendered arrangement of the music establishment and simultaneously harks back to the inspirational but heavily male-controlled girl bands of the 1960s. In addition, it may be viewed as repackaging the political momentum of women's rock and pop to mass appeal. All Saints, another extremely successful and oft-emulated girl band, are claimed to represent the 'bad' side of 'girl power'[5] and are distinct from the Spice Girls for being more obviously musically talented; yet the girl band phenomenon as a whole constructs an aspirational model particularly attractive to teens because of the glamour that embraces these pop stars. Sassiness and playful sexual poses can become an embodiment of empowerment, particularly where clothes – as in the case of All Saints and 'Sporty Spice' – are not conventionally 'feminine'. But their experiences of fame still show how women largely succeed as vocalists rather than musicians, need to have some form of 'glamour' attached to them, and have to confront institutionalised sexism at all levels of the business in order to achieve their aims.

Mainstream girlie culture, needless to say, sets great store by the visual, and its stars are young, slim and conventionally attractive, and come under quite different scrutiny in the press from their male counterparts, especially in their relationships with men and each other. It is true that contemporary boy bands come under similar scrutiny in teen mags, where they are to some extent positioned as the 'boy next door', but the mainstream adult media is more likely to concern itself with stories of internal conflicts, domestic disharmony and physical deterioration when it comes to women.

Both the Spice Girls and All Saints have black members and it is important to look at how black femininity is inevitably represented as a kind of threatening 'otherness'. In the case of Mel G, her mixed race background may always consign her to the realms of the 'scary' – rather than 'baby' or 'posh' – which quite literally suggests that she threatens at the same time as attracts men. The musical aesthetic of All Saints is more reminiscent of black soul music in its melodic harmonies, just as their street style makes fewer concessions to the demands that girl musicians be physically attractive in a conventional Barbie-doll way. Their 'badness' may partially result from this sense of their resistance to the entirely populist girl band ethos, but may also follow a more predictably racist logic which positions the black woman as the overtly sexualised image of femininity. To draw attention to difference in any way is to be pigeonholed as aggressive or having 'attitude' – never framed as desirable attributes in a woman.

Bad Girls

A more overtly political appropriation of the term 'girl' which predates the populist swell of girl power may be witnessed in the US 'Riot Grrrl' phenomenon which reached the UK in the early nineties and which owed some of its momentum to punk. Punk inspired female musicians to perform as both vocalists and instrumentalists because of the simplicity of a music where some of the major bands were famous for only having a repertoire of a few guitar chords; it wasn't that women generally couldn't play or were likely to be less skilled, but that band culture was largely masculine with very few adolescent girls picking up electric guitars or practising drums. Punk inspired a generation of performers with little developed musical skills in an environment where sophistication was a rarity. This offered women a more mainstream musical platform than the politically oriented women-only bands who emerged with second-wave feminism. Within punk, as Mavis Bayton points out, 'conventional notions of femininity were attacked and parodied by taking fetishised items of clothing and pornographic images and flaunting them back at society.'[6] In addition, Riot Grrrls generally refused to be interviewed or objectified on video, which guaranteed the impossibility of mass market success.

The Riot Grrrl phenomenon emerged from the grunge and hardcore music scene in the States in the late eighties with bands such as Hole, fronted by Courtney Love. Though feminist in sentiment, these bands tended to be rebellious against second-wave activism, arguably initiating the momentum and style of the Spice Girls and other mainstream pop bands. As Bayton observes,

> they celebrated girlishness by wearing big plastic hairgrips, slides, bunches and sports tops. The name itself speaks volumes: a recuperation of the term 'girl' against the politically correct (yet now tame) 'woman' of their mothers' feminist generation, but with a new spelling that turned it into a growl of feminist anger.[7]

Unfortunately recuperation can rapidly become assimilation and a gesture of rejection can be taken more literally as a celebration of girlishness, particularly when the spelling of 'grrrl' is lost. As we moved into the mainstream in the case of the Spice Girls, their girlishness identified their niche audience and their suitability for the consumption of pre-teens.

In Bayton's overview of women in popular music she argues that no matter how much the Spice Girls, as a dance and vocal group, can inspire young women, they don't encourage them to take up instruments and break further stereotypes about women in the music industry. She observes that 'being a Spice Girls fan leads to dressing up, dancing and singing (timeless female activities) but not playing guitar, drums or bass',[8] and this is not necessarily progress because of the way 'women's singing is seen in contrast with the learnt skills of playing an instrument, a kind of direct female emotional expression, rather than a set of refined techniques.'[9]

Successful girl band members also have to conform to fairly strict measures of conventional attractiveness, just as Madonna's superstardom has meant increasing attention to her body shape which, as she has aged, has become more muscular and athletic. Despite Geri Halliwell's assertion that 'none of us are conventional beauties,'[10] it is accepted that the Spice Girls were originally selected to form the band because of their looks, and are therefore 'likely to be viewed as "puppets" for male producers...whether or not this is actually the case'.[11] As Germaine Greer observed, this is particularly true for feminist commentators: 'feminist responses to the Spice Girls depended on whether their activities were perceived as self-regulating or whether they had been manipulated into acting out a marketing concept. In millennial society, alas, you can't have one without the other.'[12]

Here Greer hints at a marked schizophrenia in the way feminist critics have viewed female successes within popular culture: on the one hand one wants to view high-profile public success for women as a feminist victory, particularly in its potential to offer role models to other women, yet it is often hard to separate the terms of this success from the twin requisites of glamour and bodily sexual allure. With depressing regularity feminists will conclude evaluations of prominent female figures with the observation that their success depends on some kind of collusion or some Thatcherist assimilation of patriarchal principles. This is only depressing because it would be hugely liberating to be unerringly positive about the legacy of someone like Madonna, but this simply is not possible.

Madonna comes to stand out as an exceptional figure in the music industry, with little sign that multitudes are now able to follow in her footsteps. Her image, particularly during the first decade of her career, was both sexy and shocking, but it was her 'sexiness' which prevailed. For Camille Paglia, 'Madonna is the true feminist. She exposes the puritanism and suffocating ideology of American feminism, which is stuck in an adolescent whining mode. Madonna has taught young women to be fully female and sexual while still exercising control over their lives.'[13] Many others have been impressed by the control she exerts over her own business interests, but this all too easily lapses into a recognition that it is her body which is a vital component of her success. We are, perhaps, harder on women in industries such as popular music and entertainment, who tend to fit the glamour mould and whose success can only really be measured in material terms and in terms of the breadth of their fame.

Girl Power

Whatever their relationship to feminism, the Spice Girls acknowledge their legacy to it in their declaration that 'feminism has become a dirty word. Girl Power is just a nineties way of saying it. We can give feminism a kick up the arse. Women can be so powerful when they show solidarity.'[14] It is interesting that, although 'feminism' is the word to be rescued from derogatory connotations here, it still needs a 'kick up the arse', which will somehow show female solidarity. Too many people share the view that feminism (or feminists) deserve a kick up the arse – rather than the anti-feminists and backlashers who made the word dirty in the first place. This comment, which seems genuinely intended as a gesture of pro-female solidarity, shows how girl power as a rhetorical device is all too prone to appropriation for essentially patriarchal ends. It inevitably promotes the widespread view that feminism is nothing but a tangle of infighting factions who never gave serious consideration to the idea of female solidarity.

Much of girl power seems to involve meeting aggression, particularly sexual aggression, with similar aggression – like the archetypal 'ladette' who adopts traditionally 'male' behaviour in an attempt to subvert or deflect male lechery. Yet coupled with this macho inflection, girl power seems to recognise the age-old strengths of women's friendship and community and is particularly positive towards mother–daughter relationships. As Jude Davies remarks, the Spice Girls' first single, 'Wannabe', 'pivots between heterosexual romance and same-sex friendship',[15] and confirms this sense of tension between heterosexual romance and female community.

At its worst the rhetoric of girl power adopts the traditional view of women as the hidden power behind the family, and rather complacently hints that women are a priori the stronger sex who simply need to flex their muscles more publicly and persistently. This may be attractive in an aspirational way for young women – particularly in its combination of glamour and arrant consumerism – but it is hardly likely to prepare them for the gritty realities of the job market. Perhaps this sounds too wildly prosaic a deflation of a slogan which has certainly captured the imaginations of teenagers for the last few years, but at present it does project the life of the successful girlie in a social vacuum. To tackle men 'on their own terms' may also be to risk violence and peer marginalisation; and to accept male terms is to submit to a reality where our aspirations have to be reframed to suit a world which has largely operated in the interests of men.

The Spice Girls at their height offered a vision of success, youth and vitality to the young in a world where youthful, childless, sexually attractive women are the most visible fetishised image of femininity; the Spice Girls as mothers, or unmistakably ageing into their late twenties and thirties, may find that they encounter structural inequalities which are more resistant to brash aggression.

Advocates of girl power, if we can take the Spice Girl 'manifesto' seriously, seem either unaware or unimpressed by second-wave feminist arguments which claim that structural gender blindness disables women from achieving equal status to men even if they attempt to make a bid for power on male terms and without disrupting the status quo. Arguably it is the Spice Girls' difference that has catapulted them into a superstardom unattainable to a contemporary boy band; every time they assert their ability to establish themselves despite being 'girls', their girliness is what situates them apart. Their material wealth might mean that they have the last laugh, but the idea that their success can be extended to a model of girl power for all fails to take into account the fact that existing structures thrive on the exception which blurs the norm.

Young women themselves seem aware that girl power bears no relation to the 'bigger' issues, but none the less seem to hang on to the individualistic address of the slogan – 'It's about what *you* want. It's time to give men a wake-up call. We aren't going to sit back and let them have it all their own way any more.'[16] Another young woman argues that 'in the absence of anyone else girls my age could look up to, the Spice Girls became obvious role models';[17] this is partly a reference to the much-hyped 'ordinariness' of the Spice Girls, but perhaps reinforces the notion that what most young women aspire to is their success and media stardom, rather than their individual styles.

The Spice Girls, in common with 'new' feminists everywhere, seem to have forgotten, or remain blissfully unaware of, the social and political critiques offered by second-wave feminism, which tends to be simplified into a movement which went too far. Typically, their favoured feminism is that which achieved basic rights and gave white middle-class women the strongest profile to lobby for further legal and policy changes within the status quo. As Geri Halliwell observes: 'I don't really know that much history, but I knew about the Suffragettes. They fought. It wasn't that long ago. They died to get a vote. The women's vote. You remember that and you think, fucking hell.'[18]

Of course her closing expletive is ambiguous when set down in writing; she may be using it to express amazement, but it

could equally signify disbelief at the lack of progress made since
the early part of the twentieth century. In fact, suffrage *was* a
long time ago and the heroic suffragist image harks back to a
historical moment colonised only by the middle-class white
woman, almost devoid of sensitivities to class and especially
race. Nowadays, the 'exceptional' women are still far more likely
to be white women, and those black women who do achieve
success, like Mel G, may have to be careful about how they
express their feelings about racism and identity in case they are
too 'scary' for a complacent commercial media.

The entertainment industry, in common with soccer, has its
black superstars. As role models for young people they are
applauded, but once they draw too close attention to the way
racism affects such organisations, the industry backs off.
Similarly, some white women see a world of powerful women
reflected in their own image and celebrate universal 'girl
power', without a thought for its racist underside. Again, racism
becomes the sole problem of those who suffer its effects, just as
feminism is women's gripe with the world and treated with
some tolerance offset by lashings of reductive parody and ironic
'humour'.

Girl Power! is a 'manifesto' in the loosest sense in that although
it contains nothing resembling a political programme, it
encourages young women to follow their own aspirations and
seek self-definition by example. It is also a confessional in the
old style of feminist discourse in that it purports to reveal the
'truth' about the Spice Girls (including a sense of the rigours
and monotony of an average working day),[19] suggesting, as
celebrity profiles always do, that they are just like 'ordinary'
girls. There are no clear directions at the end, but its readers
know what to do next: when you turn to the final page the
'secret' of girl power is ultimately revealed – merchandising.
Girls will emulate the Spice Girls through costly mimicry
rather than doing it for themselves; the band's celebrated

diversity in their personal styles and the way they dress doesn't obviously filter down to their fans. Even the poster for sale on this page suggests that the band has submitted to an acceptance of some deeper-rooted homogeneity as they pose in identical red bathing suits – the trademark of the *Baywatch* 'babe', universally derided as lech-fest TV.

Role models are normally those who inspire others to excel in their chosen field; but this homage that manifests itself as imitation does nothing to dismantle the association of female success with a very rigid definition of femininity. Worse still, it does nothing to reassure young girls about their bodies; perversely, starvation becomes a message of empowerment to these young people as they make the association between stardom and skinniness.

One of the Lads?

The term 'ladette' is arguably a male invention, a mere appendage to the lad, expressing the view that young women can behave as badly as young men, but it also crosses over with the term 'girl' to suggest empowerment through assertiveness.

In a 1993 edition of *FHM* magazine an article called 'The Seven Deadly Sisters' featured the ladette as one of six varieties of women with whom one shouldn't have a relationship (in one sense reading this is a refreshing change from the women's glossies, in that men are advised to extricate themselves from dysfunctional relationships: in the world of women's magazines, readers are regularly instructed to change themselves rather than their partner). The article asserts that being a ladette is about being able to turn masculinity against itself, in that the female is able to appropriate so-called 'politically incorrect' language and behaviour without that enabling her male companion to do the same. In other words, 'women who are one of the lads are the men we're supposed not to be.'[20] There would be nothing particularly liberating about such a persona – part exposé of men's worst machismo, part attempt at appropriation of behaviours traditionally proscribed to women – yet it is an image which the mass media have toyed with to varying effects.

Everywoman's account of the ladette suggests a more radical effect, that it 'has unleashed a whole new range of gender behaviour',[21] linking this to changes in female behaviour as charted by a Demos survey in 1996, which suggested that women were becoming more aggressive. Yet again, this apparent shift in attitudes towards the worst examples of masculinity is hardly positive or life-affirming and suggests that although many women have profited from social and economic changes over the last couple of decades, other feminist ideals about re-envisioning gender roles and behaviours are left behind. A more cynical view is that women can get on only by adopting the worst excesses of so-called male behaviour, a strategy that tends to mean that feminism is rarely translated into work practices and does not benefit other female colleagues.

Channel 4's *The Girlie Show* became one of the more visible platforms for the ladette, in many ways offering the defining image for the end of the millennium. A *Girlie Show* producer, Courtney Gibson, argued that 'women have always behaved like this, they just haven't done it on TV before'.[22] It is difficult to determine which aspect of 'girlie' behaviour is to be lauded, but outspoken independence all too often deteriorates into pointless vulgarity without any 'political' edge. The magazine format of *The Girlie Show*, which was first launched on Channel 4 on 26 January 1996, demonstrated a clear emphasis on the look of the show rather than its content. The three original presenters – Sarah Cox, Rachel Williams and Clare Gorham – were young and glamorous, and regular features such as 'Toilet Talk', focusing on drunken young women talking about 'willies' in nightclub toilets, seemed to commit the show to utter superficiality. Other features such as 'Readers' Husbands' (a play on the 'Readers' Wives' features in some soft porn magazines) confirmed the view that this was mimicry of laddism at its most pointless.

Channel 4's press material flaunted these presenters as 'babes', describing the programme as 'spiky, Amazonian and in yer face',[23] yet it seemed to display women's ultimate weakness rather than strengths – of being perceived only in relation to men or elements of 'male' culture. Another Channel 4 programme, the shortlived *Pyjama Party*, capitalised on the pre-pubescent connotations of the girlie, featuring women dressed in nightwear indulging supposedly feminine fantasies in front of a studio audience – at best a space for the expression of separatist female culture, but one which also offered a return to girlhood as a remedy for contemporary ills.

Both shows attempted a reversal of gender roles in their depiction of men as the objects of desire, but both proved only that in order to undermine dominant stereotypes of what constitute masculine and feminine behaviours, one has to do much more than simply reverse the equation. In the same way that draping a naked man on a car is unlikely to increase its marketability, shows such as these fail to recognise that while women are primarily prized and displayed for their looks, their brashness is indulged as part of their overall sexiness. More recently, Denise Van Outen's rise to fame as ladette par excellence in *The Big Breakfast* and then as presenter of the audience-based show about sex, *Something for the Weekend*, demonstrates how thin the line between ladette as sassy, intelligent, independent woman and ladette as glamorised 'tomboy' really is. As van Outen says of herself, 'I'm a dolly girl, a real dolly, girly, girly girl';[24] and her 'look' is a direct throwback to the saucy *Carry On* females such as Barbara Windsor. These shows, figuring men as the central topic of conversation, cannot fail to depict women in relation to men, undermining contemporary female assurances that glamour and style are done 'for myself' and not for male approbation. It may be true to some extent that women have always behaved like this, getting in league with other women to enumerate the flaws of their male partners, but this has surely never been a recipe for liberation or empowerment.

Sugar and Spice?

Girl power most certainly caused some kind of quake among pre- to early teen girls in the latter half of the nineties, but it is difficult to gauge the difference between the solace young girls find today in girl bands compared to those of the sixties, since contemporary media trend-watchers are always too happy to construct a fanfare around a small ripple. Until these young women enter the world of work or of higher education it is difficult to know whether the rhetoric of choice, control and empowerment will have any lasting transformative effect. At the moment its visible effects are the most obvious ones and they seem in sum to offer a reassertion of traditional models of femininity, with younger and younger girls showing more and more of their prepubescent flesh decorated by fake tattoos.[25]

Teen magazines, criticised in recent years for their sexual explicitness, perhaps offer evidence of how girl power has filtered into the teen consciousness, yet from the ones I have studied there are no images of empowerment. To take three examples, *Mizz* is aimed at pre- to early teens, *Sugar* at teens, and *Minx* late teens. None devote much space to aspects of young women's life not associated with boys and looking good, how to fill in the time between dating boys with make-up and beauty tips (including how to depilate for girls who probably have next to no body hair), celebrities, soaps and very occasional soap box moralising.

Health education in the 28 July to 10 August 1999 issue of *Mizz* amounted to eight things you didn't know about smoking, and advice to a 'worried Michael Owen fan', who thought she might become pregnant through heavy petting, to 'take your time and don't feel pressurised into doing anything you aren't ready for'. In many ways *Minx* does read like the logical extension to *Mizz* – its total elision of the world of work in the September 1999 edition suggests its pure teen focus, with only a greater emphasis on celebrity interviews, soaps, beauty, fashion and the addition of sex, travel and health (of the rather 'exotic' kind, such as colonic irrigation). *Sugar*, a monthly like *Minx* and which claims to be Britain's best-selling girls' magazine, has a younger readership and relationships with boys tend to be described rather disingenuously in terms of snogging. Sexual matters only really feature in the problem page, or by extension in its features, such as the one in the September 1999 edition about a 17-year-old who had her baby at home ('I almost gave birth in a loo!').

Even though there are token references to female friendship, the magazines, just like the *Jackie* of my generation, emphasise fashion, beauty and boys. Fear of being different and non-conformity are constant laments in the pages that deal with embarrassing moments. These magazines offer little support to the ideals of self-determination and autonomy, setting much greater store on fitting within society's ideal. If anything, attitudes to boys are less healthy, if that could be possible, than when I was young, and life is generally described as one long scramble to get a 'lush lad'. Both titles, *Minx* and *Mizz*, promise an irreverence and feistiness which they never deliver − and, like the title *Sugar* implies, they are all syrupy and rather unwholesome.

In my reading of girls' magazines I would have to agree with Germaine Greer, who declares that 'the British girls' press trumpets the triumph of misogyny and the hopelessness of the cause of female pride'.[26] All girls' magazines seem to do is prepare children for the world of glossy women's magazines which will open up further vistas of anxiety about one's body, one's boyfriend, one's lifestyle, one's attitude. It would be conceptually naive not to understand that magazines, dependent as they are on advertising revenue, need to trade on a sense of lack; but it also explains why they never extend beyond the 'girl power' model of feminism. No wonder young girls' lack of self-esteem or ambition is reaching epidemic proportions and their search for control prompts more regular descents into eating disorders and self-mutilation. As Greer gloomily observes, 'Given the universal awareness of young women as bodies rather than people, it is inevitable that their impotent rage be turned against those bodies, which they are wilfully destroying, even as they are most admired.'[27]

'Sexism's Been and Gone!'

Girls are neither passive receptacles for everything they read in magazines nor willing and uncritical absorbers of Spice-Girl speak, and it is clear that teen magazine editors also aim to act responsibly when it comes to matters of sex and drug abuse. It is also tremendously encouraging to see girls' academic success soaring. Similarly, the Spice Girls are themselves undoubtedly hardworking and successful women. Yet what the media makes of these phenomena and how they are hijacked as symptoms of female empowerment is pure patriarchal recuperation. To use the example of the privileged few such as the Spice Girls and Madonna to suggest that all women have 'arrived' is to deflect discussions of how far women as a group have still to go. It is a strategy which gained in popularity after the arrival of Margaret Thatcher as Prime Minister in 1979, when thousands of women were silenced by the observation that, now we had a woman prime minister (not to mention a Queen!), women could rise no higher.

Women in high places, whether politics or popular music, find themselves under the kind of scrutiny that, obsessed as it is with the effect of 'masculine' power on femininity, must find a fatal flaw. Margaret Thatcher, cited as the original Spice Girl by Geri Halliwell, endured the effects of such scrutiny. Thatcher's 'crime' (among others of closer concern to feminists but beyond the bounds of this particular argument) was to have an excess of both masculinity and femininity. When it came to budgetary discussions she liked to picture herself as a housewife in charge of a large but finite purse and she always carried a handbag; in *Spitting Image* iconography, she was strutting, business-suited and physically huge against her cabinet colleagues.

Since 1998, when the government's Women's Unit suggested that the Spice Girls could provide positive female role models for young women, the Spice Girls' haloes have been slipping. Halliwell left the band that year and rumours circulating ever since suggest a direct clash between her and Mel G, pointing to cracks in the 'sisterhood' which were delightedly leapt upon by the press. Reports that Mel G's marriage was in trouble added further fuel to the press interest and the implicit suggestion that female empowerment and marital bliss might be incompatible. Yet their potential as role models, particularly in a health education capacity, continues to be exploited. With two members of the group now mothers, their ability to influence young women was further harnessed by the National Childbirth Trust to promote National Breast-feeding Week in May 1999. Mothers were exhorted to follow the examples of Victoria Adams and Mel G and, rather than focusing on the beneficial health effects for babies, breast-feeding was packaged as all the more attractive because it supposedly helped you get back into shape.[28] National television news also saw fit to set up a grand debate about the fact that Victoria Adams chose to take David Beckham's surname (although Mel G(ulzar), formerly Mel B, did the same thing less publicly), supposedly as a means of testing contemporary attitudes to feminism but in the process revisiting the ancient debate about whether women should take their husbands' names.

Girl power might indirectly offer some girls the will to pursue their dreams, but it is not a political interpretation of feminism, which is why the media love it. While these celebrities' personal choices are used to misleadingly check the political temperature of contemporary feminism, we know that we remain at the centre of a backlash.

No discussion of girl power and its relationship to feminism would be complete without mentioning Barbie, who has been associated with tutoring young girls into the ways of femininity for many years. Barbie has at times been the bugbear of feminist critics because of the adoration she inspires in young girls (manufactured by slick advertising and well-chosen accessories) and because she becomes the archetype of a feminine beauty which is physically impossible to attain – her legs are disproportionately long; her waist is improbably small and her breasts are pneumatically taut. Yet Barbie has succumbed to changes and as the 'average' women's vital statistics have changed so have Barbie's – slightly.

In 1999 she took on a new 'feminist' edge as Mattel joined with a New York group, GirlsInc, to promote a publicity campaign with the slogan 'girls rule'. The campaign aimed to donate money to programmes which educated girls about technology, science and sports. This suggests a wonderful postmodern fusion of capitalism and philanthropy, where a company exploit their girl-identification to virtuous ends and in return perhaps get the odd feminist mother to believe in girl power, doll-style. Such nineties schizophrenia may help a toy company boost flagging sales whilst seeming to have a social conscience, but it still leaves the 'girl' market of body consciousness undisturbed. From Mattel's point of view their market is not threatened and could produce another generation of well-heeled Barbie-buyers.[29]

Feminism has always shied away from spokespeople precisely because figureheads are destined to become regarded as representative of the whole movement. Yet the mass media yearn for someone to provide them with the necessary soundbites when women's issues are being discussed, and perhaps new generations of women, if my students are anything to go by, long for a role model with satisfactory feminist credentials who could regularly produce something that passes for cogent discussion on news programmes and daytime TV.

At the moment the focus on sexy young celebrities is reassuring for those who find self-proclaimed 'feminists' threatening, because although these stars represent success (often measured materially) and empowerment (often measured by the breadth of their fan-base), they also visually offer an adherence to and belief in traditional femininity. At the level of body image, 'girl' power is not ultimately a radical assertion of gender difference which extols the virtues of biological femaleness; it is a deep and uninterrogated pleasure in girliness à la Barbie. The girl's-lavatory humour that was encouraged on programmes such as *The Girlie Show* is an empty and defensive assertion of solidarity, a whitewash which encourages more and more young women to believe the myth that 'sexism's been and gone!'[30]

Chapter Three
Lads: The Men Who Should Know Better

The magazine *Loaded* single-mindedly pursues the new lad motif to its extreme – he is almost always white; part soccer thug, part lager lout, part arrant sexist. This combination of 'attributes' is knowingly offensive, particularly in its sexual objectification of women, yet the popularity of such laddish literature has grown exponentially over the last decade. In 1998, circulation figures for three of the most popular magazines – *Loaded*, *Maxim* and *FHM* showed an increase of 3.6 per cent, 29.2 per cent and 16.7 per cent respectively (July–December 1998) and although recent Audit Bureau of Circulation figures show a drop for some magazines (*FHM*, *Loaded*) others are on the up (*GQ* and *Maxim*). Overall title circulations are still much larger than they were three to four years ago. Just what is it that makes these knowingly offensive stereotypes so appealing to so many men, and, for that matter, a significant number of women? And, in the golden age of irony, how can we reply to offensive material without that criticism being deflected as humourless nitpicking?

In *Loaded*, the lads' frame of reference is very clearly demarcated – sport, pop, alcohol, soft drugs, heterosex and soft porn. Further, this is the domain of the male and the male alone, where women function only as objects. The gang mentality of this new/old masculinity is studiously exclusionary and even intimidating to any stray woman reader – particularly in the letters page, which ranges from lavatorial humour to descriptions of sex as the act of silencing shrill women. The letters page of the May 1997 edition, for example, contained the following: 'Whatever happened to that annoying bird Sarah from Clevedon – who kept writing in to beg for a shag? A Good Work Fella! *Blue Peter* badge to whoever finally managed to shut her up by giving her a proper seeing to!'[1] Where women figure as part of a feature, it rapidly becomes apparent that the report's main focus is the woman's body and her sexuality, divorced from any real consideration of her other attributes. An article on Helen Mirren, for example, is framed by seven photo insets, six of which feature Mirren nude or semi-nude. The brief text assures us that 'Mirren is a lot more than just a bit of middle-aged crumpet,'[2] although her age and her 'crumpet' value are of course the only focus of the piece. Regardless of endless debates about the relationship of images to our 'real' lives, this sample article tells us everything we need to know about the *Loaded* response to women and invites a feminist rebuttal which yet appears redundant because of the blatant offensiveness of the piece.

These magazines forestall all hint of a dialogue about how women might feel about such images by sidestepping the language of soft porn with a matey 'humorous' tone. If anything, all consciousness of their retrograde sexual agenda is obscured by a 'dumbed down' approach to the issues they deal with. *Loaded* in particular self-consciously establishes a masculine personal space which fences off feminist criticism and politics, delighting in its retreat from outside accountability. In the case of men's magazines and other manifestations of lad culture such as TV, it appears that populist feminist debates have been scrutinised and found wanting. However, I would contend that part of the irony of laddish productions is that they depend on a familiarity with feminist rhetoric whilst seeming to sidestep it altogether. Sean O'Hagan, writing in 1991 in *Arena*, says of the 'new lad' that

> this half-(new)man, half-lad is a tentatively positive reaction to three decades of feminism . . . In short, he is well versed in the language, and protocol, of post-feminist discourse and he will never, ever, even after a few post-prandial brandies, slip into Sid the Sexist mode like a regular (Jack the) lad might. Of course, he may tell the odd dubious joke, but he'll preface it with the words, 'You'll probably think this is a bit sexist, but it's dead funny,' just so you know that he's aware that he isn't trying to be New Mannish (i.e. boring, right-on), but is actually acutely aware of, and can even relish, his ideological shortcomings. And besides, the joke *is* funny.[3]

Despite the fact that I believe that contemporary lads *do* leap on the chance to slip into Sid the Sexist mode, this is an interesting articulation of the new lad. The lad, repelled by the new man persona which he regards as boring and unattractive to women, makes a joke about his contradictory relationship to feminism and in doing so abdicates any responsibility for his own sexism. Feminism is emptied of any significance beyond being associated with a bunch of dour ageing women who only want to spoil men's fun. But many of these jokes are only funny when set in a context of presumed ideological disapproval – the Millie Tant to their Sid their Sexist. It is a sense of 'naughtiness' which perpetuates the will to tell sexist jokes rather than the quality of the jokes themselves, and perhaps in an environment where alternative comedy has lost its shock value or is simply considered old hat, new humour is just a reinstatement of the same old chestnut.

Men Only

Tim Edwards, in his analysis of masculinity, style and consumerism, *Men in the Mirror*, asserts that 'If men's style magazines respond to anything in sexual politics then it is the undermining of definitions of masculinity in terms of production or traditional work roles, and a deep seated set of anxieties concerning the lack of future focus for young men, which has almost nothing to do with reactions to second-wave feminism and almost everything to do with the fear of unemployment.'[4]

There is much evidence in recent years that men as a group are feeling more disenfranchised by increased unemployment, and the figures for incidences of violence and suicides among young men are frighteningly high. The popular press speak of the 'feminising' of the workplace as one cause of increasing male unemployment, clearly signalling that the more women make up a significant part of the workforce, the more men have to pay. As we shall see in Chapter Six, men are undergoing a crisis in the way their identity is defined, and this crisis is alleged to be directly related to female emancipation. Feminism is roundly viewed to be at fault. Whilst it is true that new lads are assuredly the product of identity crises, it is not just that generated by feminism, but also by gay liberation and anti-racist movements, which act as a reminder of what mainstream male culture, such as big budget competitive sport, regularly excludes.

The term 'new lads' suggests a transition from the past conventions of masculine behaviour but also a kinship with 'new man'. The new man, of course, never existed – he was a media vision of what pro-feminist men would look like and was usually sent up as dull, ineffectual, emotional and possibly effeminate. It is therefore not surprising that we see elements of this negative reaction coming across in men's magazines.

Sean Nixon argues that what was distinctive about the early general-interest men's magazines such as *Arena* and GQ in the mid- to late eighties was 'the sheer volume of visual representations of men. From adverts for clothing and toiletries to celebrity portraits, the magazines were a bulging visual parade of masculinities.'[5] Yet the slick grooming and style awareness of the new man of the eighties did, as Nixon points out, leave an area of sexual ambivalence with a blurring of the boundaries between the gay and straight male look. He goes on to document a shift in editorial policy on behalf of GQ, who are 'proud to announce that the New Man has officially been laid to rest (if indeed he ever drew breath). The 90s man knows who he is, what he wants and where he's going, and he's not afraid to say so. And yes he still wants to get laid.'[6]

It is possible that eighties style magazines opened up opportunities for new definitions of heterosexual masculinity which drew from feminist critique and gay male style, but that the resulting new-man image didn't quite add up for most straight men. Indeed, Tim Edwards suggests that the near-pornographic depictions of women and sex is a kind of antidote to the homoerotic potential of the style and fashion features which displayed the male body for a male gaze,[7] and this obviously in part explains the increase in 'glamour' shots and copy reinforcing the heterosexual message.

Another more disturbing aspect of this heterosexual imperative is that men's magazines currently seem able to attract huge numbers of celebrity females prepared to strip off and/or adopt a porny pose for the lads. Katharine Viner cites examples of Ulrika Jonsson chained up (*Loaded*, May 1998), Zoe Ball in leather and high-heeled boots (*Esquire*, December 1997–January 1998) and Helen Baxendale made-up and in suspenders and black lace (*Esquire*, May 1998), observing that 'In the 1970s, when women started to complain about the way they were represented, it was nameless centrefolds who spouted these kinds of sentiments, who appeared desperate to show and tell the world how much they loved sex. Today, it is women who are famous for other things, for, you know, non-sexual things.'[8] She goes on to lament the means by which women respected by other women as successful in their fields are turned into static images which scarcely resemble them and which make many women uneasy.

Of course, as Viner points out, any objections could be

deflected by the observation that these individual women participate of their own free will and may indeed enjoy the experience; yet one can only lament the increasing correlation of the image of the successful woman with the sexy one. It is also assumed that the woman being photographed is the only one who may or may not be offended by it – just as Madonna's 'control' is held to guarantee the liberatory potential of her output – yet the impact is altogether different when one encounters these images bedecking magazines, pop videos, books and television in many different formats. As Viner says, we had the language to reject images of anonymous females in soft porn and characterise them as exploited and/or brainwashed, but what do we do when the faces are famous and remind us that women have entered domains far removed from the sex industry?

It is difficult to explain the rise in such depictions and their subjects' seeming collusion in them; placed in the lad mags in particular they are like a lewd gesture directed at the women's movement and its call for women be judged for what they are rather than what they look like. They guarantee that women will continue to enter the public world on male terms and be subject to its sexism. Even though it is distinctly unfashionable to say as much, many women will pay the price for the way some celebrity women choose to display their fame. It is not, and has never been, a question of whether individuals should have the right to use their bodies and themselves in whichever way they choose; it is not a question of whether people should or shouldn't have the freedom to enact their own sexual fantasies and desires: it is a question of who is responsible for the image which results, which in its homogenisation and its predictable range of varieties suggests repression and even oppression far more than it suggests liberation.

Boy-zone?

Although I agree that there appears to be a staunchly heterosexual defensiveness in *Loaded* – since lads and style don't really seem to go together, yet homophobia is distinctly uncool – I would argue that there is another dimension. Not only do these lads seem to be unreconstructed men shoring up their masculinity, but there is also a celebration of the boyish which enables another form of nostalgia and which results in endless references to 'trivia' from the seventies and eighties. In its launch issue in April 1999, *Loaded*'s elder 'brother' magazine, *Later* (devised by IPC to reach a slightly older market) contains articles on Barry Sheene, James Hunt, Bruce Lee, Clint Eastwood, the film *Rollerball*, sex symbols of the sixties and an article in which the reporter is made to act as if he were fifteen years old again.[9] This boyishness is echoed on popular TV in *Men Behaving Badly*, *Have I Got News For You* and *They Think It's All Over*. Women who guest on the latter two shows rarely come off well and are regularly effectively silenced by the men – often to service a 'gag'. Accordingly politics and sport are seen to remain the province of men to which women can only enter at the risk of becoming the butt of sexual innuendo.

These programmes clearly foster a boyish gang mentality. In the case of *Fantasy Football League* this is exacerbated by the visual and verbal inclusiveness of the studio audience, who chant and demonstrate their sporting loyalties by wearing their team's football shirt. In the case of the quiz show *Have I Got News For You* the team captains engage in verbal sparring and series in-jokes with a verbal virtuosity reminiscent of schoolboys with their own private mode of discourse. This sense of 'community' is perhaps one response to the idea of the male identity crisis, in that it offers a powerful sense of belonging to a group which has its insiders and outsiders. Like schoolboys too, the new-lad brand of humour depends upon showing celebrities failing in some way, so that *Fantasy Football League* shows footballers humiliating themselves and focuses on sporting mishaps rather than football's 'golden moments'. At times this light-hearted ridicule threatens to take a more offensive turn, such as the send-up of then Nottingham Forest forward Jason Lee. This involved depicting a number of footballing gaffes whilst representing him by dressing up a presenter in blackface and using a pineapple to denote his braided hair style.

There is also a clear manifestation of what can only be termed a renaissance of Benny Hill style 'naughtiness' in these programmes, and nostalgia is certainly a significant feature of such shows. But it is a nostalgia which does not necessarily equate with any perceivable period in history: 'Nostalgia is not just a sentiment but also a rhetorical practice. In the imaginative past of nostalgic writers, men were men, women were women, and reality was real.'[10] Its main purpose is to discredit any perspective which threatens to shatter complacent conservatism – and lad culture is militantly conservative about women, as well as defensive about the traditional qualities of the male. In the case of lad mags there is not only nostalgia for images of women in the mode of *Playboy* at its heyday, but also the desire to utter all the offences known to man, freed from the imagined tut-tutting of 'ardent' feminists. Men's magazines celebrate images which three decades ago feminists would have denounced without hesitation; but these contemporary images are set in a context which attempts to deny us the right to have any opinion at all. The subtitle of *Loaded* is 'for men who should know better', and those that 'know' better are not only male readers aware of the embeddedness of their own history within the histories of the women's, gay and anti-racist movements, but feminists who should, it is implied, know better than to complain.

As Cosmo Landesman laments, the new generation of men's magazines never lived up to their promise of offering a style journal with real articles (which leads him, in the company of others, to mourn the passing of the old-style *Playboy* or *Esquire*). Landesman concurs with the view that all these mags offer is 'an escape route back to the comforts of boyhood; a sunny space full of old football heroes and "tasty telly totty" of the 1970s.'[11] He rightly points out that while 'magazine woman' was the object of an extensive critique from the Social Affairs Unit for portraying women as self-centred and obsessed with sex, 'magazine man' has no redeeming features, since there is barely an aspirational level to this identity on offer. While women's glossies do encourage the philosophy of self-improvement which stretches slightly beyond the makeover and multiple orgasm, the men's mags promote the egocentric drive for instant gratification.

Landesman's view, which is shared by others, is that the launch of *Loaded* in 1994 began the downward shift in quality which is not only witnessed by the babes-and-breasts design of such mags, but also by the endless recycling of celebrity stories and profiles. Despite the sense that these magazines insult the intelligence, over 1.5 million men buy them every month.[12] Somewhere along the line it is as if 1.5 million men are basking in reflections of their own dumbing down as part of a refusal to examine their most deep-seated prejudices against women.

The increase in popularity of men's magazines is not solely a British phenomenon. Although *Loaded* has a very British feel about it, most notably in its schoolboy vulgarity and problematic relationship to male styling, there is evidence that the lad mad is gaining some purchase in the States, with *Maxim* spawning a brother edition over there. The babes-and-booze angle is absolutely identical, yet the sports and fitness section shows cultural variations, as does the relative lack of vulgarity in the form of scatological humour and seventies TV and soccer trivia. I don't have enough recent experience of American culture to judge how widespread the 'lad' image is, although it is well known that school and college fraternities generate a culture of 'jockism' which mixes sporting prowess with celebratory sexism. For Susan Faludi, the US version of *Maxim* 'helped its lads to imagine they were hunters once more, their prey the opposite sex'.[13] With circulation figures of 950,000 in the spring of 1999 and another magazine, *Details*, following suit with the leadership of *Maxim's* previous editor, it appears to be a strong contender in the men's magazine market. Faludi certainly suggests that the refocusing upon female bodies as an antidote to the homoerotic narcissism of the men's style magazine is compatible with similar shifts in US culture as a whole.

Irony and Offence

Lad mags and popular entertainment are fascinating because in many ways they operate on the basis of radical uncertainty about the composition of their audience. The producers of programmes such as *Fantasy Football League* and *They Think It's All Over* are probably young enough to have worked in mixed environments where there is an awareness of sexual politics and 'political correctness'. Similarly, they must know that the audiences for these programmes are mixed. Yet there is no attempt to incorporate a female perspective and the terms of reference and subject matter are almost exclusively aimed at young white heterosexual males. It is difficult to determine how female members of the audience are supposed to respond to a particular brand of joke that takes women as its target and often belittles women's participation in sport. These jokes often take on a direct and lovingly sexist slant, but they do so ambiguously, with an iconoclastic sense that they are retreating to some previous (but perhaps more easy and comfortable) male identity. Classic notions of distinctions between the sexes appear to be reinforced, but it is never easy to determine to what extent parody and irony support or undermine those distinctions.

Irony of course provides the perfect opportunity for linguistic ambiguity, since you can be seen to project a particular point of view only to claim distance from, or even opposition to it. The nineties might be characterised as the decade of irony. As political integrity and sincerity retreated from the realms of mass culture, we were left with 'knowing' and playful images and gestures which profited from the more populist aspects of postmodernist thought.

Postmodernism emphasises the intertextual and multi-referential aspects of cultural productions and consumers/readers/viewers are credited with increasing levels of sophistication as they find themselves viewing films, encountering advertisements, watching TV drama and light entertainment which endlessly refer to other films, ads and TV shows. Postmodern thought has been popularised to suggest that images generate a range of meanings and that the spectator plays a crucial role in creating their own individualised understanding of what they see. Perspectives such as feminism conflict with this view in their insistence that some meanings – particularly those attached to representations of women – are entrenched in the images because of visual conventions which are tried, trusted and repeated endlessly. To take an example, we instantly recognise the Page 3 pose because it has become so inscribed in our consciousness through repetition. Any play on or manipulation of such a pose will therefore have resonances of its original context. Critics would argue that the pose can be used ironically, playfully and can even deconstruct the original meanings of the image, therefore generating completely new inflections on an old standard. Feminism is accused of seeking univocality in its unfashionable obsession with meaning and interpretation in a quest to eradicate sexist images. Because of this, feminism becomes regarded as oppressive to ordinary people who don't want to feel patronised by someone else telling them what the advertisements, their magazines, their favourite TV programmes are 'really' saying.

But the new irony makes it difficult to object to *anything* potentially offensive, as was seen in the case of complaints against two recent television advertisements for Scalextric and Nintendo. The Scalextric advertisement featured a father in a maternity ward telling a newborn child about the joys of Scalextric when he is interrupted by a nurse telling him to put the boy down and play with his own daughter. The slogan 'Scalextric. It's a boy thing' is astonishing in its bald chauvinism, rivalled only by Nintendo's 'Willst thou get the girl? . . . or play like one?' used to market the game 'Zelda'. More astonishing by far is the Independent Television Commission's response that 'such tongue in cheek treatments were unlikely to have the widespread negative effect that those who complained feared',[14] putting the burden of proof on the recipient of the message rather than recognising its clear and baldly stated intentions.

Women are, of course, accustomed to these kinds of pronouncements, where unless offence can be 'proved' in some nebulous way it is assumed that such messages are harmless and not to be taken seriously. The problem is that possible effects are infinitesimal when taken as isolated examples, but potentially explosive if one could measure the cumulative effect of such advertising added to women's experience of sexism and inequality in our culture as a whole.

This small but concrete example of advertising suggests a sea-change in the way charges of sexism are responded to from the days when feminist groups were able to exert enough pressure to exhort the creators of such material to rethink their marketing strategies. The advertisers are presumably assured that such a stance will not affect their sales and will hopefully boost them in an arena where gendered toys appear to be on the increase. Two things are clear from this example: a belief in the plurality of ways a message can be received makes it very difficult to level charges of sexist intention against the sender; and as long as the message is intended as a 'joke' no one can touch you for it.

Jokes and feminism are popularly considered to be incompatible, but for radical feminists such as Robin Morgan, writing in the 1970s, sexism is all-pervasive and includes 'everything from the verbal assault on the street, to a "well-meant" sexist joke your husband tells, to the lower pay you get at work ... to television commercials, to rock-song lyrics, to the pink or blue blanket they put on your infant in the hospital nursery'.[15] In other words, the 'trivial' was the first stop for second-wave feminists precisely because images and soundbites of the world around us matter; the ideology of male supremacy persisted after the enfranchisement of women by just such means.

The Robin Morgans of this world were castigated for taking 'rational' feminist arguments, such as the right to vote and receive equal pay, and lowering the tone of the debate by introducing such trivia as the stuff of everyday life. In reality, scrutiny of such trivia is uncomfortable because the possible consequence is that people might have to police their language or think again about what a certain image 'says'.

After a short honeymoon period people got fed up with so called political correctness as if it were a rather unpleasant trend – like puffball skirts – and now those who draw attention to the way images can perpetuate the consciousness of gender, racial or other inequities are seen to be the 'thought police' who rob individuals of their freedom. Feminists assert that language and intention as well as behaviour matter: since this implies that men in particular have to modify their attitudes, it is hardly likely to be popular.

In today's consumer society, advertisers seem to be falling over each other to produce provocative and risqué images. It is telling, I think, that the backlash against feminism has been most pervasively at the level of a war of words, even when material gains for women seem to suggest positive progress. One is also left wondering whether this new frenzy of political incorrectness will result in more provocative and offensive images around race.

Naughty But Nice?

Comedy series with an anticipated mixed audience such as *Men Behaving Badly* do in many ways feel like the direct descendants of *Whatever Happened to the Likely Lads?* since classic sitcom tensions are played out. The men want to slob around, go to the pub or be promiscuous and the women are looking for a sensitive lifelong partner who can help around the house. Yet new lads programmes focus much more keenly on the flaws in masculinity as it is currently constructed, tantalising the audience with the implied suggestion that things could be otherwise.

In *Men Behaving Badly*, Gary and Tony are seen as being plagued by insecurities and anxieties about masculinity and taking on a 'male' grown-up role, which lies only partially submerged beneath their laddish persona. These insecurities are usually displayed in their relationships with women, whereas their most appalling behaviour is triggered by the proximity of other lads. Sitcoms have always specialised in exposing such tensions, but contemporary ones are more likely to explore them overtly and will be less likely to restore 'order' in the re-enactment of clearly defined parameters of 'male' and 'female' behaviour. None the less, these shows still retain their investment in a classic notion of femininity and the image of feminism shown is always a parodic one in which the woman is always victorious because she is always right. In truth, however, the women are the losers. Dorothy and Deborah, the female characters in *Men Behaving Badly*, are portrayed as always wanting to change their men, yet in the face of complete stasis they are willing to compromise by making the best of their choice of men, which rhetorically involves indulging their naughtiness. The message is, it's better to be with the lads than be single.

Comparing this comedy with US TV imports, it is hard to determine whether this particular lad image would be intelligible to an American audience. Certainly, the success of *Men Behaving Badly* prompted a US version, but it flopped badly. Caryn Mandabach, president of Casey Werner, the company that took the format to the States, explains it thus: 'in the US, men in their 30s who live together are not lads, they are homosexual. We over-estimated our ability to sell the concept of lads to the American public.'[16] Yet *Friends*, of course, has two men living together and its comic thrust, which depends partly on our recognition of ourselves or our partners in the characters' behaviour and situations, is echoed in *Men Behaving Badly*.

The naughty-lad image filters from the style magazines to the sitcoms to the minor TV celebrities to the consciousness of the target audience. This persona, unlike the 'new man' which mainly remained shorthand in the world of the media for a particular masculine style, has affected men's perception of women just as assuredly as it has borrowed its lad accoutrements from the world beyond the media.

The Frank Skinner Show, a chat show hosted by the comic and erstwhile co-host of *Fantasy Football League*, explores some of the tensions in lad-scheduling as well as suggesting an almost seamless link between the agenda of the show, the lad mags and popular commentary on women. He interviewed the TV presenter Gail Porter after her nude body had been projected onto the Houses of Parliament in 1999, signalling quite clearly that his main interest in her recent career was the provenance of these photographs and her assurance that she had no problems with being naked. The interview seemed to encourage her to signal her enjoyment at posing nude so that the impact of the pictures was individualised rather than exposed as part of a tendency to exploit the female body for male ends. His interview with Germaine Greer on 13 May 1999 had, unsurprisingly, little to do with the substance of her recent work. Given that she doesn't fit the youthful glamour mould of Gail Porter, Tara Palmer-Tomkinson and Zoe Ball the interview seemed to be more about the need for men to reassure themselves that powerful, successful women, especially feminist ones, are not too scary. Disappointingly, when he attempted to parody a feminist intellectual perspective, Greer rather kindly allowed his stumbling attempts space without making him look even more ridiculous. His references to her age (particularly the 'joke' of offering her a bag of Werther's Original sweets) also seemed to be about defusing her power.[17]

Everything about the new lad suggests anxiety about the future of the male in a world where feisty women seem to be multiplying, perhaps explaining the fervour of attempts to reduce such women to pin-up status. *Frank*, the women's magazine that in its launch issue in October 1997 described itself as a 'candid, no-bullshit take on the way we live in the 90s', ran a feature on laddism, noting that it had moved from the margins to being 'the reigning cultural role model'.[18] Ian Penman suggests that the impetus behind laddism was an ironic generational shift in the late eighties 'to retrieve sex-as-fun from the shadowlands of HIV',[19] which has dissolved into soft porn. He too laments the slow spiral towards a mass cultural quagmire where men are 'offered few other ways to think or behave or negotiate their lives',[20] suggesting what is abundantly clear – that there is an absence of social responsibility among media trend-setters about the consequence of the lad image.

Suzanne Franks seems to support this view of laddism, arguing 'that as women's identities have broadened and encroached upon male territory, instead of swapping and merging of identities, men moved further into the traditional heartlands of male identity – the drinking, shagging, sporty stereotype.'[21] Julie Burchill implies laddism has a pathology of its own closely associated with the acculturation of men into a life of being serviced by women, so that 'social circumstances had conspired to let him stay young for longer until he reached the point where manhood looked dead scary and infanthood seemed the ultimate in blameless, shameless thrills'.[22] I think she has a point; one factor in the massively increasing popularity of these magazines must be their incessant childishness and their will to dumb down worldly issues to the common denominators of sex, drugs and rock 'n' roll. Women are encouraged to view this behaviour as naughty but nice, the harmless teasing of men who just haven't grown up.

Real Men

'Lads' as represented on TV by presenters and charismatic actors have nothing to do with the laddism of 'the streets', which has none of the badinage of the TV interview but masses of woman-hatred for free. Suzanne Franks argues that 'the stars of New Laddery are symbolic of the problem. Comedians, footballers and pop stars are very much part of the winner-takes-all society of sharply rising inequality where the incomes of the top earners have soared to the stratosphere'; all, as she suggests, 'far removed from the real male losers'.[23] In a way, the lad on the street is disenfranchised by his own lad heroes whose massively inflated salaries serve to underline the growing chasm between the lifestyles of the rich and poor, and where few men are likely to realise their aspirations as devil-may-care media lads. For some of these celebrities their laddism seems to be a means of holding on to their 'working class' credentials, but like any kind of nostalgia, it is safe basking in the rosy glow of the unreal. The real lads on the street are presented with an identity and a set of behaviours which encourages childish irresponsibility and growing alienation from 'real' women, in the belief that this is aspirational – after all, it works for the most popular DJs and football stars of our time. In truth such men have the luxury of revelling in this neanderthal behaviour precisely because of their privilege.

Meanwhile, real men, when questioned about their attitudes to rape and violence against women, show some rather shocking attitudes to real women. Research carried out by the Edinburgh Zero Tolerance group[24] claimed that one in two men thought that raping a woman might in some cases be acceptable, one in five men thought that forcing wives to have sex would be acceptable and one in ten men would rape if they could remain undiscovered. Add to this the finding that one in three women thought that in some cases it would be acceptable for men to force a woman to have sex, and you have a set of responses that are depressingly compatible with the responses to women expressed within lad 'fantasy' culture.

Dave Hill, speculating on the future of male sexuality, says 'all the old absolutes, all the tired prescriptions will finally be revealed as false and it will be increasingly accepted that there is no such thing as a pure masculine sexual identity; that heterosexual and homosexual are not polar opposites, the one "normal", the other an offence against nature.'[25] Yet we have no representation of the redefining of gender and sexuality in any of the men's magazines or male-oriented TV broadcasting which have developed since the eighties; neither do women's glossies spend much time offering up models of male behaviour that transgress the tired old norm. So in the present day, as Dave Hill also acknowledges, 'the advance of male immaturity is apparent everywhere',[26] and feminist critiques will have to redouble their efforts to resist the seductions of irony and parody.

Lad culture signals better than anything the growing impatience with feminism's demands on men and, in Rosalind Coward's words, they no longer respond to such demands with 'genial masochism'.[27] In truth, feminism never came up with a convincing version of how men could change in line with female transformations, not least because they felt they'd had enough of 'servicing' men. Men may change, according to Paul Wallace, author of *Agequake* (1999), purely because in future years there will be a woman shortage and they'll have to clean up their act. Yet such predictions are no comfort to women who, in the wake of some material shifts in the realms of employment and politics, are witnessing very little obvious change in men's consciousness of what their future social role should be. In fact, lad culture at every level suggests an aggressive refusal to endorse or acknowledge any changes in the relations between the sexes, their wallowing in dollybird nostalgia a clear indication of what they really, really want. For new and post-feminists the answer is to include men in a movement that may not even have to call itself 'feminist' anymore.

Chapter Four
New Feminism, Post-feminism and Feminist Revivals

Contemporary society, perhaps more than ever before, is a society in which marketing concepts reign supreme. Brand awareness is everything in the race to persuade the consumer to sign up for a particular product. But, as we will see in this chapter, the importance of labels and presentation can also be applied to ideologies, as 'New Labour' realised to great effect in their campaign for the 1997 General Election. In terms of modern feminism we have seen the emergence of new feminism, post-feminism, power feminism and women-centred schools of thought which reject the label of feminism altogether.

'New' and 'post' are prefixes added to the term 'feminism' when the writer or speaker wants to make it clear that they have a certain antagonism to the term, because of the connotations it generates, or because feminism by itself is seen to be inadequate to their own definition. Prefixes such as 'power' are also added to imply that feminism will be overhauled and made over with a new sense of direction. All imply that the word feminism is not enough to embrace their own political programmes or personal agendas, and that it has been manipulated to certain ends from which they want to exclude themselves. But as with most additions of prefixes, the central concept remains the same, so that 'new' and 'post' imply cosmetic changes rather than radical rethinking. Feminism is portrayed as a territory over which various women have to fight to gain their ground; it has become so unwieldy as a term that it threatens to implode under the weight of its own contradictions. This also implies, as the work of Christine Hoff Sommers suggests, that feminism can be 'stolen' from its 'rightful' owners and made to mean something altogether different.

The most undignified thing about contemporary feminists, therefore, is that they fight; and two women fighting, even if it is only verbally, tends to draw a cluster of spectators revelling in this unseemly display. One such 'fight' allegedly took place between Camille Paglia and Beatrix Campbell in December 1997, hard on the heels of an in-print spat between Germaine Greer and Suzanne Moore. As Rosalind Coward observes, commenting on the Paglia/Campbell exchange, 'whenever [feminists] open their mouths, even to get an old grudge off their chest, they are taken to be staging a bitter no-holds-barred fight for the soul of feminism itself.'[1] Conflict is used as an easy way for critics to question the credibility of feminism as well as to confirm the average observer's belief that to be a feminist one has to be slightly unhinged. Conflict certainly underpins Fay Weldon's depiction of the rise and fall of a feminist publishing company in *Big Women* (1998) and the TV adaptation screened in the same year visually underscored this. No conflict is ever seen as developmental or healthy, but rather as evidence for detractors who wish to position feminism as dogma which stultifies rather than stimulates debate.

Feminism, leaderless as it always has been, never satisfied the public's thirst for figureheads and spokespeople, and therefore the media made figureheads for themselves, usually forcing one feminist to take the adversarial position against another. Other than producing some entertainment for the media, events such as that featuring Paglia and Campbell are hardly likely to be sites of productive discussion, since it is rare that deeply held beliefs or crucial issues are debated. It is of course likely in the case of these spats that a great deal of media stage-management or manipulation is involved and this contributes enormously to their superficiality.

Camille Paglia is popular because she can be relied upon to be both controversial and utterly convinced of her own importance as a modern cultural theorist. She was in this case quick to over-react, with retorts that sounded rather childish in print: 'British feminism has not produced a single idea, a single book, a single personality that has had international impact since the great Germaine Greer – who is Australian.'[2] Paglia, always fond of hyperbole, located feminist struggle as locked between various nationalities and here perhaps betrayed the parochialness of her own perspective which, while making great sweeps in cultural and historical terms, is relentlessly monofocal.

For many, evidence that feminists fight is proof that feminism in its current state is decidedly unhealthy. Some modern liberal critics such as Christine Sommers offer a nostalgic view of authentic feminism to suggest how far 'we' have strayed as a result of second-wave radicalism: 'Credos and intellectual fashions come and go but feminism itself – the pure and wholesome article first displayed at Seneca Falls in 1848[3] – is as American as apple pie, and it will stay.'[4] For Sommers, feminism has been hijacked by militants who have muddied its peerless homegrown reputation. From her nostalgic perspective feminism should be comforting and homey, part of the status quo and therefore a natural bedfellow of high liberalism where any talk of a 'sex war' would be the result of mischief by radicals. Not only is this a very partial view of the scope of feminist thought, but it is also a rather imperialist one, which sees feminism as originating from the USA, the standard bearer for the 'real thing' across the globe. Sommers adopts a perspective of one who knows her feminist history; as someone who has witnessed the madness of the sixties and seventies, but has the clear-sightedness to take us back to 'the pure and wholesome article'.

While liberals like Sommers would reject the second wave for its radicalism, a new wave of younger feminists are inclined to characterise it as puritanical or joyless, and feel that in order to inject a new vivacity into the issues a kind of feminist iconoclasm is healthy and even liberating. For Angela McRobbie this iconoclasm is equivalent to generational conflict between a younger and older generation in order that the new may establish an independent identity. She remarks that

> Coming across as loutish and laddish is a provocation to a generation of feminists now established as figures of authority... They have to develop their own language for dealing with sexual inequality; and if they do this through a raunchy language of 'shagging, snogging and having a good time', then perhaps the role this plays is not unlike the sexually explicit manifestos found in the early writing of figures like Germaine Greer and Sheila Rowbotham.[5]

For McRobbie the main difference between the two 'generations' is the younger feminists' use of populist language directed at 'ordinary' women. The use of raunchy language, though it may be evidence of generational rebellion against the old feminist order, does not of itself offer radical social critique. There may well be power in the use of irony and playfulness to argue a 'feminist' position, but once the rebellion is over, there is a need to identify what connects or separates different wings of feminism.

The purpose of this chapter is to suggest that while contemporary iconoclasm may be refreshing, it is not necessarily a new thing, and offers no insights into what younger women feel to be the central social and political problems confronting them today. Moreover, criticism of the 'mistakes' of the past only contributes to the misconception that feminism has nothing to say to women in general. It is unfortunate but true that many women feel alienated from the language and jargon that feminists use, even when they may be deeply sympathetic to its sentiments. Regrettably, the most widely available feminist voices are still those of white, formally educated women, which further entrenches this sense of an unfathomable chasm between privileged women and everyone else.

The rhetoric of feminist debate is unfortunately still fragile enough to be derailed and used in ways that can be both offensive and banal and this can have the effect of trivialising its basic precepts. Nowhere is this clearer than when feminist responses to overtly sexualised images of women are discounted as pure prudishness; but also the concepts of freedom and choice, so intimately connected to visions of social transformation, have come to be identified as purely individual 'lifestyle' statements. The repackaging of feminism (as 'new', 'post', 'power' and so forth) is not of itself destructive; but it does add strength to the arguments of those who wish to undermine feminist calls for change by severing its links to more overtly political forms. As I pointed out in Chapter Two, the reason the media love 'girl power' so much is probably because it is so anodyne. Yet, paradoxically, new feminism borrows most of its language, its ideas and some of its agendas for change straight from the works of its foremothers.

Mothers and Daughters

The whole history of the development of second-wave feminism is one of conflict, disavowal and moving on. For this reason alone it is not always clear what the fuss is about when some new young woman offers her own critique of the movement. What is more perplexing is when one account becomes a bestseller, as in the case of Naomi Wolf's *Fire with*

Fire (1993), while another merges more comfortably into the background, as did Maureen Freely's *What About Us? An Open Letter to the Mothers Feminism Forgot* (1995).[6] Wolf's work offers a broader sweep, but its success was also a success in product marketing, which capitalised on Wolf's glamour and media-friendliness. The book was marketed from the outset as a controversial critique as well as an accessible and intelligent guide to the fundamental issues confronting young women today, particularly those who feel that their generation has no voice in the feminist 'orthodoxy'.

Freely offers a critique 'from within', to some extent, characterising herself as one of many women who experienced their feminism at the sharp end, and now sense that they belonged to a 'generation of warrior guinea-pigs'[7] who participated in a movement that did not anticipate the massive shifts that would occur as huge numbers of its members had children and began to perceive their 'choices' in entirely different terms. Here I believe that Freely taps into the suspicions of many women that feminism only 'works' when you're unattached and relatively unhampered by other personal and professional obligations. For Freely, as the more personal parts of the book testify, the reality of motherhood made her realise the ephemeralness of freedom even today. She felt that feminism had not prepared her for this, arguing that 'the ideal reader for a feminist blockbuster is a university student whose beliefs are in disarray after a few months without parental guidance, and who is desperate for a more exciting, more accepting guide to explain the world to her'.[8]

Freely's anger is also directed at the new feminists such as Naomi Wolf and Katie Roiphe and media figures such as Camille Paglia. Although for personal reasons I find myself sympathetic to Freely's claim that feminists, especially the charismatic 'superstars', have strenuously avoided tackling motherhood – or rather the heady mixture of personal and social meanings which become attached to it – I don't experience their work that way myself. I am more interested in Freely's claim that contemporary feminists have 'locked us all into adolescence'.[9] In a collective fear of turning into their mothers, these feminists, Freely argues, avoid the subject of maternity entirely, as if they were to remain perpetual teenagers. This offers some insight into the way that the endeavours to make feminism 'new' are always the province of young women, just as 'girl power' and other popular expressions of female empowerment only seem to address the adolescent.

For Freely, the prejudice against mothers and the practical problems of motherhood are 'the central problem of modern feminism',[10] which needs to broaden enough to consider the means by which men and women can bring up their children without one becoming an economic dependant of the other. In contrast to Freely, Melissa Benn sees in past feminism a different ambit: 'Far from a monolithic rejection of motherhood, or even a buried dislike of the process, there is a constant tension between an urge towards separation and connection.'[11] For Yvonne Roberts, conversely, it is fathers and fatherhood that have been omitted in feminist writings: 'In contrast, there is any amount on mothers... The father remains faceless, without character, known only in the negative, symbolic, of course, of the patriarchy.'[12]

Women like Freely and Rosalind Coward, all too familiar with the peaks and troughs of the women's movement, are examples of the way gaps and silences are rooted out of feminist thought and new dimensions are added in. This is clearly a productive way forward where criticism offers the opportunity to consider deficiencies in previous arguments and supplement them with fresh ideas – hopefully gesturing towards a shared conviction that while feminism continues not to reach the majority of women, it is always a work in progress. To take a metaphor from women's craft, it is a patchwork of ideas with the stamp of many individualities impressed upon it; so why do some young feminists see it as a ready-made orthodoxy?

New Feminism

Naomi Wolf is one such writer who pits feminist struggle as one of youth against age. Here the youthful feminist rebellion is described in terms reminiscent of McCarthyist witch-hunts: 'My friends and I are all self-defined feminists. But we know that if we were to stand up and honestly describe our lives to a room full of other feminist "insiders" – an act that should illuminate the route to female liberation – we could count on having transgressed at least one dearly held tenet on someone's list of feminism's "do's" and "don'ts", and being called to account for it.'[13] If feminists such as Wolf really do see second-wave feminists as Big Sister it is not surprising that younger women feel rebellious. But also implicit in this statement and the argument which follows is the idea that such feminists are in a direct way hindering the fight for female equality by trying to keep their troops in order and gratuitously prolonging an 'anti-male' stance.

Wolf implies that a new generation of women are mature enough to deal with sexist innuendoes and jokes without recourse to the militancy of classic radical feminism. This may be the case, but this example plays directly into the hands of detractors, since it uses one of the most popular criticisms of feminism – that 'older' feminists had no sense of humour. This claim for modern female fortitude simultaneously infantilises feminist forebears (who clearly weren't able to take a joke) and is reductionist in its suggestion that feminists might feel that one of the main problems confronting women was how to navigate their way through sexist jokes. Above all, Wolf sees feminism's primary role as enriching the individual's life by offering women the freedom to make personal life choices; any broader areas of social or ethical responsibility are very much marginalised.

Feminists who continue to advocate the need for social transformation and hold on to the unfashionable view that women still face deeply entrenched inequality in material and ideological terms are seen as dangerous ideologues who disguise the 'fact' that women have already won their corner, and in their intellectual work contribute to the cultural impoverishment of today's students. More recently it is rare to find a high-profile new feminist who declares her own political position, promoting the idea that the perspective she puts forward is more natural and 'common-sensical' than that of a woman who prefaces her statement by saying she is a radical feminist. The straight-talking common sense of new feminists is assuredly attractive, and appears to make their work more accessible, but it tends to obscure their personal agendas in putting forward these ideas, just at the tendency to suggest inclusiveness may marginalise the experiences of women from different backgrounds.

Young new feminists come in several varieties, but Naomi Wolf, Rene Denfeld and Natasha Walter all believe that the second wave has lost some of its relevance to a new generation and that it is in some way repressive to women.

Denfeld, who I discussed at length in Chapter One, is most extreme in her criticisms and simply denounces the older generation of feminists as New Victorians; Wolf in *Fire with Fire* (1993) argues that the 'genderquake' has arrived, and feminists have been slow in capitalising on the new opportunities it provides. Her vision of 'power feminism' intends to do just this through the encouragement of the acquisition of power, particularly financial power; and her rather individualised model of feminism tends to foreground the needs of a middle-class constituency, even though she latterly talks of the importance of small support groups.

Natasha Walter, a British journalist writing about her book *The New Feminism* in the *New Statesman*, sees the newness of this brand of feminism lying in the widespread absorption of feminist ideas even among women who do not willingly call themselves feminists, arguing that 'if feminism is to consolidate its mainstream appeal, it is time to bury some of the old myths about feminists. Time after time when I talked to young women about feminism they expressed unease about identifying with a movement that is still seen as being puritanical and man-hating.'[14] Yet Walter herself seems to subscribe to some of these myths about feminism, and perhaps does not pay enough heed to the way certain aspects of modern feminism have been reinterpreted, or misinterpreted, in negative terms. Again, feminism is to blame, rather than those who have distorted its message. Primarily Walter feels that 'this generation of feminists must free itself from the spectre of political correctness',[15] and disengage the personal from the political – a link which has always been at the heart of feminist politics. For her, feminism's assertion that the personal is political resulted in undue scrutiny of individual women's private lives and this leads Walter to conclude, in common with many others, that feminism has operated as a constricting ideology.

She is particularly exercised about the imposition of a feminist dress code which she claims denied women the right to enjoy the act of adornment, but omits to clarify that protests directed against certain archetypes of femininity emerged during the late sixties and early seventies when particular dress codes and modes of feminine behaviour were insisted upon. She seems to forget that there was a time when jeans and shirts or dungarees and no make-up were a shocking rejection of this, rather than the feminist 'uniform' they came to be seen as. Take, for example, Germaine Greer's argument in *The Female Eunuch*, published in 1971: 'Most women would find it hard to abandon any interest in clothes and cosmetics, although many women's liberation movements urge them to transcend such servile fripperies. As far as cosmetics are used for adornment in a conscious and creative way, they are not emblems of inauthenticity: it is when they are presented as the real thing, covering unsightly blemishes, disguising a repulsive thing so that it is acceptable to the world that their function is deeply suspect. The women who dare not go out without their false eyelashes are in serious psychic trouble.'[16] Greer distinguishes between the act of adornment to enhance the personality and that which attempts to push the individual into an acceptable feminine mould.

Personalising the political, as it used to be understood, was also a way to show women that their own experiences were relevant within women's history of oppression and that they were not alone; it was a way of declaring that some of the most important issues confronting women took place in a space marked off from the rest of the 'real' business of the world. The family and sexual relationships were traditionally demarcated as a space safe from public scrutiny, where a man ruled supreme; feminists wanted to point out that it was similarly a place where no one could hear you scream and where the law would rarely intervene. From later arguments in *The New Feminism*, it is clear that Walter understands all this, but she chooses to pick up on confusions and anxieties generated within feminism and the women's movement, particularly around guilt associated with having relationships with men, and tends to make them into feminism's defining moments.

At her clearest Walter is arguing that feminists must move away from identity politics and into a politics which seeks equality, because in common with all new generation feminists, she believes that equality and integration into what already exists is preferable to revolution or further conflict. But casting Margaret Thatcher as 'the great unsung heroine of British feminism'[17] is hardly building up a view of a future feminist politics with equality at its core; to equate Thatcher so directly with feminism is far more problematic than simply recognising that her success has made a huge difference for women today to the point that she may be a role model of sorts. To be fair to Walter, she sees her own articulation of the new feminism as feminism in movement and lists five goals at the close of her book, which are 1) to address inequality in the workplace; 2) to devise a new strategy for childcare; 3) to gain men's involvement in the home; 4) to investigate the poverty trap and offer specific help; and 5) to provide support for women who experience violence.[18]

Books such as Walter's are important to the survival of feminist politics because her work is accessible and does appear to speak to a new generation keen to understand how feminism relates to their lives. Her optimism for the future is infectious; it is just regrettable that the feminism of the future is being built upon a certain amnesia about the past.

Rene Denfeld similarly makes suggestions for the way forward, and although she does not have faith in large organisations, she suggests that small groups could work on issues such as childcare, contraception, abortion rights, political parity and sexual violence.[19] Not only are the aims of these two women extremely similar (although Denfeld makes no direct mention of poverty and neither explicitly addresses other forms of oppression), but they have striking similarities to the 'Four Demands' devised at Britain's first national women's conference in 1970, which were equal pay, equal education and opportunity, twenty-four-hour nurseries and free contraception and abortion on demand.[20] It is perfectly understandable that young women are frustrated with what they see as the difficulties of translating ideals into large-scale activism, but they would be wrong to think that they were the first to experience such frustrations. They are at the latter stages of a movement which discovered that revolutions require a shift in consciousness, but that consciousness is the hardest thing of all to shift. Progress has certainly been made on all the original four demands, but those issues become more complex on closer investigation. Arguing for equality itself is a tricky issue when women themselves are unequal at so many levels, and because, more importantly, it is sometimes necessary to argue for the particularities of being female – for instance, in identifying how pregnancy and childbirth affect a woman's presence in the workplace.

Many new feminists can be distinguished from 'older' ones by their faith in the possibility of integrating feminist demands into the political status quo. Melissa Benn, on the other hand, characterises feminism as an 'unfinished revolution' which began with Mary Wollstonecraft's *Vindication of the Rights of Women* (1792), suggesting the need for further radical shifts in the political and social balance. She argues that 'a culture of contentment has crept into feminism'[21] within which hard political issues such as poverty, racism and the sexual division of labour are supplanted with feminists in the 1990s 'writing less about the world than about *reflections* of the world'.[22]

I would argue that reflections of the world can be very telling about how people perceive their own conditions of existence, but it is clear that what Benn fears is the construction of a feminism which focuses on the world empty of social radicalism and seemingly peopled only by the white middle-class contented few who have managed to forge a certain degree of equality in their own domestic and work contexts. Certainly these criticisms could be levelled at aspects of the work of Natasha Walter; despite her chapter on working-class activism and her push for action at the close of the book, it is clearly aimed at readers whose world is comfortable enough for them to be more incensed by the idea of older feminists telling them what to wear than by a wider world which still prevents women's full participation in social and professional life.

Today there is necessarily a tension between the rhetoric of choices and the drive to continually identify the means by which oppression is perpetuated, and feminists, after the stalemate of so many clashes over identity politics, have yet to find a way to get around this. For Walter the politics of the personal have become too involved in scrutinising the feminist quality of people's private lives and the new feminism she envisages is not so much an identity in itself, an ideology which colours one's entire life, but rather a politics which should be taken up or discarded depending on whether it helps you make sense of your own feelings of inequality. Here we find echoes of the rhetoric of girl power which implies that style is itself a gesture of empowerment.

None the less, Oona King probably echoes the sentiments of many when she identifies the virtue of new feminism as being that it 'explicitly offers something to men as well as women'[23] in its acknowledgement of a world where changing professional identities necessitate a re-evaluation of life in the home. New feminism can be challenging and its belief in a feminist future is heartening. At its worst it exploits the most archetypal and ill-thought-out criticisms of feminism – particularly around its alleged puritanism – and is not always clear to signal its own indebtedness to the fundamental precepts of second-wave feminism, or to make clear that these issues have been kept alive entirely by the commitment of these self-same 'puritans'. In sum, new feminism, though a tad disingenuous about what it owes to past feminism and how 'new' it really is, is perhaps preferable to what has been termed 'post-feminism'.

Post-feminism

My thoughts on post-feminism have changed little since I wrote *Modern Feminist Thought* (1995); where I felt that the prefix 'post' signifies 'going beyond' and 'discarding the essence of' whatever the declared intention. Needless to say, many 'post-feminists' deny that these meanings form any part of their use of the term, but there is a clear attempt to create a separation between feminism's 'political' identity and its more 'academic' theoretical one, which suggests that the politics somehow could be optional.

Sophia Phoca, one of the authors of *Introducing Postfeminism* (1999), expresses the hope that 'postfeminism is considered as a different manifestation of feminism – not as being anti-feminist'[24] and suggests that the post-feminist perspective is that put forward by a younger generation of women, adding weight to the association of 'post' with 'going beyond'. Here lie the germs of an assumption that feminism has achieved some of its major aims and that post-feminism might be, therefore, more about offering contemporary society a little fine-tuning in a final dissolution of patriarchy.

Writers such as Ann Brooks would, however, reject any implication that post-feminism is apolitical, arguing that it 'is about the conceptual shift within feminism from debates around equality to a focus on debates around difference. It is fundamentally about, not a depoliticisation of feminism, but a political shift in feminism's conceptual and theoretical agenda.'[25] Such debates around difference are in part about recognising that women are divided by race, class, culture and sexuality, as well as – in a more philosophical vein – arguing that the category 'woman' is unstable as an identity partly because of these differences. Mature feminism has long since recognised the impact of difference upon the category 'woman', but would none the less claim that it is still vital to refer to women collectively because of wider experiences of oppression which are shared.

In *Introducing Postfeminism*, post-feminism is located in the development of French feminism and psychoanalytical and post-structuralist theories which have emerged since the 1960s, and although this is not clearly stated, it signifies a fragmentation between theory and 'politics', or issue-based thought, culminating in 'case studies' of artists such as Cindy Sherman, who are offered as examples of post-feminism but with no clear link to the theory outlined.

Post-feminists who are involved with modern theoretical developments in the fields of postmodern and post-colonial thought argue that the 'post' signifies engagement with feminism rather than rejection of it. Beyond the will to claim 'theory' for one segment of feminist thought, and to reinvent a discourse which suits a younger generation of women in all its multifaceted glory, I remain unconvinced that post-feminism is a necessary or illuminating term. It is, as Brooks acknowledges, eagerly grasped by the media to confirm fragmentation, intellectual exclusionism or political inertia within sexual politics, and for that reason alone should be treated with some scepticism. For all its exposure of race and class hegemony within feminism, I see little evidence of self-conscious interrogation of its own theoretical bases along such lines and have yet to encounter, for example, a post-feminist account of race. It could unfortunately be the case, as Myra Macdonald remarks, that 'postfeminism takes the sting out of feminism,'[26] and for Michèle Roberts, 'post-feminism comes to mean unthreatening, nice. Less a politics than a behaviour.'[27]

For Melissa Benn, post-feminism (interpreted by her as the conviction that equality exists) is narrow in its scope, particularly in regard to the realities of motherhood: 'if feminism opened the Pandora's box on these demands and painful emotions, post-feminism slammed it shut again. Post-feminism is self contained to the point of amnesia and arrogance.'[28] At its worst, post-feminism reinforces many women's suspicion that feminism has no relevance to their daily lives or ordinary concerns.

Post-feminists often like to present themselves as bad girls rebelling against dowdy feminist mothers, in the same way that new feminists depict collision between old and new feminism as a symptom of generational conflict. I guess on one hand the construction of old feminists as mother-figures is interesting in light of post-feminism's embrace of psychoanalytical theory. Old style feminism again becomes the unwelcome conscience of womankind, the dispenser of trite aphorisms which encourage only victim identification and moral purity based on the denial of personal pleasure. Feminism becomes something 'we' must be liberated from in order to explore the endless possibilities of free-floating desire – desire which is almost always linked to consumption and sexuality. In this way objects such as mainstream pornography are identified as exploring new possibilities rather than perpetuating images of sexual subordination.

Both new and post-feminism are laying claim to choices supposedly removed by feminism and if there is a popular cultural manifestation of this it may be in the sudden explosion of female celebrities displaying themselves in men's magazines (see p62) and a 'younger' generation of women who claim the right to express themselves through personal style. These debates do, however perversely at times, keep feminism alive in the popular imagination and are testament to its continued relevance – as Angela McRobbie declares: 'the strength of feminism lies in its ability to create discourse, to dispute, to negotiate the boundaries and the barriers, and also to take issue with the various feminisms which have sprung into being.'[29]

Feminist Futures

Germaine Greer, returning to the fray in 1999, clearly feels that our culture is less feminist today than it was twenty years ago. *The Whole Woman* is both a response to this and to new feminists' easy assumption that old feminists were just wrong-headed.

Her new book, neither a recantation nor sequel to *The Female Eunuch*, is wide ranging and uneven in tone, moving from highly specific examples and statistics to huge sprawling generalisations such as 'in the last third of the twentieth century more women were penetrated deeper and more often than in any preceding era,'[30] or 'every year vast numbers of women have their wombs removed.'[31] This admixture is part of its attraction, and I suspect that Greer deliberately makes it impossible or at least very difficult to agree with her on all counts. Yet her book reminds us of some marked contrasts between the new and old feminists, in its attempt at a global range, in its anti-capitalist politics and its sharp moments of clarity and anger.

Greer affirms that the 'personal is still political'[32] in her closing chapter – which, entitled 'Liberation', is itself a challenge to new feminists who are happier with 'equality' – arguing that 'equality is cruel to women because it requires them to duplicate behaviours that they find profoundly alien and disturbing.'[33] Here she shows how, in early second wave thinking, when equality was spoken of it was always analysed with an awareness of difference – the biological facts of difference, but more importantly what culture makes of these. Greer chooses to celebrate female difference here far more explicitly than she did in *The Female Eunuch* and her main point about the language of equality, particularly how it is used in new feminism, is that it signifies a pull towards masculine givens and reaffirms the primacy of male biology to dictate how difference can be interpreted.

Greer's view on men in general is often hard to assess, mainly because she primarily concerns herself with the damage that absorption in men's needs does to women. In her closing chapter she claims that 'Women cannot force a change in such male behaviour because, as the men don't care if they are there or not, they have no bargaining power'; the only solution she perceives is for 'women to make a conscious decision not to want men's company more than men want women's. If that means segregation, so be it. If the alternative is humiliation, there is no alternative.'[34] This is the kind of statement that might confirm Coward's worst fears that feminism has nothing to offer men, yet it has nothing to do with men specifically, and everything to do with observing how women perpetuate a sense of their own weakness.

Catherine Bennett, reviewing *The Whole Woman*, is irritated by Greer's eccentricities – her railing against the multiplication of laundry since the introduction of the washing machine, for instance, arguing that 'such digressions...make it difficult to read Greer's book as anything other than a grand tour of her own interests and obsessions'.[35] American historian Stella

Tillyard makes a similar point in her belief that Greer's books 'have developed into a kind of serial autobiography and they should be partly understood as such. *The eunuch* [sic.] which elaborated her own persona as a liberated woman, was followed in 1984 by *Sex and destiny*, an attack on western sexuality written when Greer, at 45, must have been coming to terms with her own childlessness.'[36]

Although it is to some extent self-evident that one's shifting experience influences one's feminist politics, and Tillyard perhaps overstates the autobiographical elements of Greer's work, this maturing second-wave constituency helps us to understand the later reflections of Greer, Freely and Coward as in some sense empirical attempts to plug some of the holes in their own earlier thinking. Greer's impassioned though sometimes unsupported assertions carry a clout that few feminists can rival. Where Greer thoroughly parts company with new feminists is in her assertion that striving for equality is ultimately colluding in a masculine world, whereas liberation suggests a female cultural future: 'liberation struggles are not about assimilation but about asserting difference, endowing that difference with dignity and prestige, and insisting on it as a condition of self-definition and self-determination.'[37]

The sum of feminist endeavour today is a heady mixture of the radical and the liberal, of equality and difference, and of some writings that seem to bear no relation to second-wave thinking at all, until, as Ros Coward remarks, referring to the sudden and suspicious renewed popularity of feminism: 'We find ourselves in a looking-glass world in which words seem to mean their opposite and in which anti-feminists are more feminist than ourselves.'[38] Greer at least has managed to survive in an arena where some of the most active figures in feminism have sunk into oblivion, such as Kate Millett, who was, in the late nineties, broke and jobless, and asked, 'why do women seem particularly unable to observe and reserve their own history?'[39]

Feminists are never going to agree on everything, but

perhaps there are new ways to disagree that are more resistant to media makeovers as 'catfights', or other such terms which imply that women can't refrain from bitchy competitiveness. Despite my reservations about new feminism, it clearly goes some way to establishing a popular platform for feminism again, even if we don't yet have what Genevieve Fox feels would inject new dynamism into feminism – 'the Bridget Jones of feminism, a cultural hit that inspires [young women] to pick up, and pass on, the feminist baton'.[40]

Chapter Five
Blair's Babes?

Just as the prefix 'new' added to feminism allowed for a certain shift in its political inflection, so Labour successes in 1997 were correlative with the addition of the same prefix. New Labour has proved profoundly popular; having dispensed with the flat cap imagery of old socialism, and the working men's club it comes disguised as a nice middle-class couple who care about society – but only the bits which directly touch their lives, or make for good press copy. With its distancing from the working-class image of socialism comes a disavowal of what is seen as its constricting ideology which would, one might think, include a dismantling of the rather masculinist image of old socialism. But it remains debatable to what extent Labour has remodelled its male-oriented image in favour of a woman-friendly one.

The official Labour Party website[1] has its own women's pages which encourage political participation at local and national levels. The website is at pains to remind women everywhere that Labour is 'listening' to them, yet while there is a push to recruit more women to the party there is scant evidence that there is any full recognition of what prevents women from being equally represented. Feminism as a tool for analysis seems to have no relevance to the approaches offered by any of the three main political parties, and is certainly not referred to in any of their websites. The acceptance that women have yet to be fully represented in parliament, figures about unequal pay, violence and so on, are instead presented as widely acknowledged but perplexing truths which can be remedied through the normal democratic procedures.

Labour's victory in May 1997 delivered 101 of a total 120 female MPs to Westminster and, even though that left them up against 539 men, it posited the possibility that women, by their presence in numbers, could enact some changes in practices that would encourage the appointment of even more. Shortly after the General Election, Kirsty Milne in the *New Statesman* called this revolution a 'triumph for quotas',[2] claiming that half of the New Labour women were from all-women shortlists (declared unlawful in January 1996). Compare this to Conservative figures, where candidates were chosen 'on merit' and there are only 13 women among 165 MPs.[3] In addition, only 3 of the 46 seats won by Liberal Democrats were won by women, mainly because they were fighting seats where the Liberal Democrats had little chance of winning and because they had not been selected to fight seats where Liberal Democrats were retiring.[4] During the 1999 European elections the Liberal Democrats did, however, head up about half the regional lists with women, which demonstrates either a significant change in policy post-1997 or, more cynically, how much less seriously the European elections are taken.[5]

Considering the means of selection of all the main parties, and now that Labour has stopped all-women shortlists, the number of women MPs could easily plummet at the next election. Equality laws have backfired against women in this major respect: positive discrimination (a policy that recognises that existing prejudices against women make fair representation of women otherwise impossible) has been outlawed. Nevertheless, it has been widely acknowledged that getting elected is the smallest of battles when one has to contend with a workplace that demands cripplingly long hours and denies the value of family or social life for anyone.

In the aftermath of the 1997 election victory, Tony Blair posed for photographs surrounded by the 101 new woman MPs. The media, perhaps predictably, seized the opportunity to give this event the 'girlie' treatment by dubbing them 'Blair's Babes'. This offensive umbrella term simultaneously homogenised them as a group and presented them as distinctly unthreatening; at a remove from real power, feminism and the old left. Also, as Jane Pilcher observed, the term implied that the 101 Labour women '"belonged" to Blair in a way that the 317 male Labour MPs did not',[6] and perhaps there is an element of self-fulfilling prophesy in this depiction of them as some kind of political 'harem' — a will for control on the part of the male-dominated media and a will on the part of New Labour to exploit this new improved gender ratio to their own opportunistic but gender-blind ends. Blair's Babes were soon to begin their 'dizzying descent to Stepford Wives',[7] where obedience to Central Office would blunt their ambition for change; like the now defunct shortlists which helped so many of them through selection, they seemed, even before they began, a force on the wane.

This was a group destined to be blamed by outsiders if the Commons wasn't immediately modernised and socialised in their wake. This conveniently took the focus off the way the political structures actually worked. Even though four-fifths of them professed themselves 'feminist' in a Fawcett Society poll carried out in the summer of 1997, they were hardly likely to feel that they should act as a collectivity on every women's issue, since that kind of protest would place gender before party allegiance. As Anne Perkins argued in the *Guardian*, 'for the newcomers rebellion would be political suicide;'[8] especially in such a centralised government.

While it would be heartening to think that such a high number of women MPs would be able to network, share

experiences and offer support for significant changes, it is
depressing that, from the outset, the 101 Labour women were
immediately homogenised in a way male MPs never would be.
For feminists, the fact of their femaleness was important, but it
is typical that their differences were accordingly played down
and certain doubts were expressed about the likely competence
of all these 'new girls' in a way that would never be applied to
men, who, if appointed, are automatically seen to be qualified
for the job. It also obscures the point that there were only two
black women appointed;[9] a fact which emphasises how the
blanket terminology obscures inequality between women from
different backgrounds. Nevertheless, it is heartening to think
that the more women present in the House, the greater the
diversity of female viewpoints that will come to the fore. In this
way hopefully women can be seen as staunch defenders of
women's issues as well as making perfectly good politicians in
more general terms.

Family Ties

It is perhaps the anticlimax following this mass entry of women
into a male bastion which has led commentators such as Helen
Wilkinson to re-evaluate the legacy of Margaret Thatcher's
Downing Street years. Wilkinson argues that Thatcher 'blurred
the boundaries between "masculine" and "feminine" behaviour
and potentially liberated us all ... to flirt with our masculine
and feminine sides.'[10] Certainly a 'free market feminism',
economically driven, could be no respecter of biological sex;
yet there remains a blindness to the domestic ties of mothers
and carers in particular which stacks the odds of success in the
market against many women. Wilkinson herself avers that
Thatcher's free market feminism was itself in tension with her
mission to restore 'family values' to an ailing British society,[11]
just as her own role as mother never gelled with her belief that
mothers should remain with their children.

Free market feminism – the concept that, given notional

equal access to the economy, it is up to women to realise their potential by competing in the modern workplace – is certainly Thatcher's legacy to women. The market, it is implied, has no gendered axe to grind and therefore women should not seek special treatment, but simply grasp the opportunities ostensibly laid out to them. It is a philosophy, in part at least, adopted by Naomi Wolf in *Fire with Fire*, whose 'power feminism' exploits the realities of advanced global capitalism. It is nakedly individualist, racist, promotes competition within a meritocracy, and, given all these things, is the stance most likely to cause more women to be downtrodden in the wake of one power-feminist success.

Thatcher's legacy to feminism is a complex one, yet it is not surprising that a woman so vilified during her prime ministerial years would now be ripe for rehabilitation. However, her rise to supreme power at the 1979 General Election is marked by the strange 'coincidence' (remembering that she had been party leader since 1975) that during this election there were fewer women returned as MPs than had been the case for nearly thirty years.[12] Furthermore, during her time as Prime Minister she only appointed one woman to Cabinet rank, Baroness Young (Lord Privy Seal and Leader of the House of Lords, 1982–3).

New Labour in its policies is supposedly increasingly family oriented, although the only real families it concerns itself with are the 'functional' ones – similarly middle-class, employed, white and heterosexual in the main. It has been noted in the past how the concept of family in all its shifting historical definitions tends to subsume the adult female. Talcott Parsons' sociological formulation of 'the family' in the 1950s still has a great deal of resonance. Here the woman is seen as playing the 'expressive' role of support and care while the husband acts as breadwinner and therefore provides the concrete and material link with the outside world. The man acts as figurehead and, regardless of shifts in employment and changing perceptions offered by feminists over the past thirty years, his presence or absence is one indicator of a family's health, in addition to his employment status. There is no awkward conception of the 'working father' – this role isn't seen to affect his position in the workplace – but there are 'working mothers' and then just mothers. Mothers aren't necessarily unemployed because they can 'choose' to be housewives; so regardless of what else women do they are ideologically charged with the maintenance of this private realm which has always had an uneasy relationship to the public and political.

Of course this image of the family exists more powerfully at an ideological level than it does in real life. It is the model we are brought up to believe is the 'norm' and therefore most 'natural' one. Yet this conception becomes less and less easy to apply to people's experiences of the family in contemporary society. What New Labour capitalises upon in their assertion of family policies is the *idea* of family, to which people have nostalgic recourse and which is supposed to represent the best chance of emotional and financial stability. As Michèle Barrett observes, 'ideologies of domesticity and maternity for women, of breadwinning and responsibility for men, are articulated very strongly in families themselves in contemporary society and it is unsurprising that feminists should have pointed to "the family" as a prime agent of gender socialisation and hence women's oppression.'[13] As Barrett and others have pointed out, the success of a certain idea of the family is the means by which certain structures can be hailed as 'natural' and common-sensical. The family is a term laden with common-sense assumptions which make all of us believe that we understand the term instinctively; therefore when Tony Blair makes his family orientation a part of his political identity we are led to feel that we share and value the same things.

Most political parties have declared themselves as 'family' parties at some time or another, and social policy has implicitly if not explicitly reflected this investment. Where New Labour differs from 'old' is that the concept has acquired within it a notion of egalitarianism (represented by Cherie Blair, her work and the Blair family); where it does not differ is in its will to excise representations of the family that don't accord with the bourgeois norm. What feminists object to is the fact that women's issues become obscured by political assumptions about their role within the family. Yet 'Blair's Babes' were held up as representative of the future for Britain's women in miniature – greater representation, diversity and listened to by men – as if from this they could represent a sea change in the position of women throughout the nation.

New Lads, New Danger

New Labour, despite its valuing of the family, remains studiously male in its orientation. There may well be more women than ever in parliament, but Blair's Babes only occasionally feature within the movers and shakers. Where they arc important figureheads, such as Mo Mowlam in her past role as Minister for Northern Ireland, they move back into the shadow of Blair at key public moments, such as the signing of the Good Friday Agreement.

As Helen Wilkinson observes, 'Blair's internal coterie is predominantly male,'[14] as is the culture with which he surrounds himself. Blair prefers football to golf for relaxation, which suggests on first sight a less elitist haven of sporting privilege and reflects the fact that more members of parliament are emerging from middle- and working-class backgrounds.[15] In addition it marks him off as distinct from his immediate predecessor, John Major, who, although from a modest background, was an avid follower of cricket. The will to create the impression of classlessness may provide one explanation for the suitability of football rather than cricket, yet football has had a middle-class facelift, courtesy of people such as David Mellor and Nick Hornby, so Blair's love of the game has little to do with supporting a working-class tradition.

Football at a professional level remains an almost exclusively male preserve, and for Helen Wilkinson, the love of football is just one more sign that New Labour has gone new lad. New Labour shares with the new lad bourgeois rootlessness: in the absence of being able to claim a working-class authenticity (even John Prescott has famously refashioned himself as middle class), football offers the lad steadfast male cultural credentials. If football is, along with babe-watching and drink, the last refuge of the lad away from feminist scorn, perhaps football allows New Labour to redefine its male appeal in the wake of a female parliamentary 'invasion'. Blair's (and Tony Banks's and Charlie Whelan's) association with the game might just be an example of how new politics fast disappears into a shade of the old. Banks's successor as Minister for Sport, Kate Hoey, has been framed in the popular press primarily by her love of football, and her appointment prompts questions about whether the new lads are under siege, or simply perceive themselves to be recruiting a like-minded ladette. Hoey, who is reported not to believe in 'positive discrimination, nor in women's ministries or female issues',[16] is going to make an interesting female role model.

It seems to be the case that New Labour has inherited the naked individualism of Conservatism in the 1980s, and refashioned into an ever greater thirst for power and centralised control. Its relationship to political realities may also be blurred, as Wilkinson suspects: 'At its worst, New Labour come dangerously close to inhabiting a world where politics itself becomes the manipulation of news copy, where the medium has become the message. The hierarchy's flirtation with celebrity culture, combined with its media addiction, already blurs the boundaries between politics as art-form and real life.'[17] This concern about media friendly policies is hardly likely to sit well with the less populist women's issues.

It may seem churlish to anticipate the likely fates of these women in parliament when second-wave feminism – in particular radical feminism – never spent much time trying to get a voice 'within' the political institutions, preferring to commit to the idea of revolution, where these structures would necessarily be dismantled. Having said that, in Britain neither socialist nor liberal feminists made much headway in their bid to make inroads into organised politics. There is no women's organisation in Britain able to parallel the scope and sweep of the USA's NOW (National Organisation for Women), founded in 1966 and still offering a national platform for women which allows feminist demands to reach the political mainstream. NOW, due to its longevity, is something of an institution and as such would scarcely be expected to offer radical politics at its heart, but it is an immensely successful lobbying organ with half a million contributing members (a figure unlikely to reflect the real number of its supporters) and hundreds of local chapters across all the US states. In their web pages they declare that among their many activities they organise large-scale protests, support the election of feminist women to Congress, champion new laws and advocate for individual victims of rape, harassment and sex discrimination. One of many individuals who testify to their support and aid is Carol Moseley Braun, the first African-American woman ever elected to the US Senate.[18]

This is a world away from the situation in Britain, where various women's organisations offer differing kinds of support to different women's-interest groups. The closest in terms of its lobbying role would be the Fawcett Society, which is a campaigning organisation hoping to raise issues of equality, influence decision makers and work with like-minded organisations. Given that there is nothing quite so high-profile as NOW, Labour's Women's Unit (strictly speaking part of the Cabinet Office), could be a huge advance for British women, although its positioning within the Labour Party and the parliamentary structure is less promising; and predictably the unit seems to have symbolic rather than actual relevance. Like the Equal Opportunities Commission, it has to be seen to be all–inclusive in order not to frighten the establishment away, but of course none of this matters if the research undertaken by the unit receives little publicity and even less supportive backing from the Prime Minister.

The more high-profile treatment of issues relating to women, such as Gordon Brown's 1999 so-called 'budget for women and children', returns us to the family orientation of all mainstream parties since time immemorial, where women's needs simply become submerged into those of the family. Meanwhile, in 1999 Baroness Jay and Tessa Jowell, ministers for women, headed up an almost unpublicised 'Listening to Women' government roadshow. Whether this will be another 'cosmetic' gesture towards women's issues, or whether it will actually result in real change remains to be seen.[19]

Harriet Harman's assurance to women, that 'we will make sure government knows and understands their changing lives and needs. We will promote family-friendly employment and an open, tolerant society with equal life chances for everyone,'[20] sounds spectacularly hollow a couple of years on when Harman couldn't even carve some 'equal life chances' out for herself when it came to her own parliamentary career. The 'powerful Cabinet sub-committee for women' to be chaired by Harman back in 1997 seems a chimera – there is no real evidence of that power in action,[21] although national strategies such as that on violence against women launched in 1998 may result in realistic drives to ensure women's safety in the home, at work and on the streets.[22] Speaking in June 1997, Joan Ruddock, in her role as Minister for Women, outlined the government's priorities in setting up their Women's Unit as comprising a national childcare strategy, healthcare, the problem of violence against women, pensions and the 'return to work' programme for lone mothers.[23] Baroness Jay, in her speech at the Labour Party Conference in September 1999, placed a great deal of emphasis on the family, returning the women's agenda to the 'family-friendly mainstream' focus of the party. The problem of this specific association of *women* with the family yields the inevitable conclusion that families are women's problems, and women's individual identities disappear. This may work at an emotional level, but in political terms it predictably makes women's lives the 'problems' that need to be addressed by legislation, rather than the institutionalised gender blindness of politics, work and family life. (Interestingly, in her attempt to deny the laddishness of the parliamentary Labour Party, Jay refers to herself in terms of her family relationships, arguing, 'I may be a grandma rather than a lad, and may not know every football result, but I'm certainly not excluded.'[24])

Two years on, few women in Blair's government have managed a high-profile stance on women's issues, although Harriet Harman has succeeded in rehabilitating herself to some extent as a supporter of parental leave. Melissa Benn argues that once 'both the standard-bearer and symbol of New Labour woman . . . Harman's treatment at the hands of the New Labour lads has made her rather more, not less, of a feminist heroine.'[25] Unfortunately suffering at the hands of the mainstream is always likely to create easier sympathies amongst other feminists.

In the main many feminist commentators feel that Labour is exploiting the happy accident of this massive increase in women MPs to its own insistently patriarchal ends. Germaine Greer asserted in March 1999 that 'the most immediate and effective enemy British feminism has is the Labour Government, which points to the number of women Labour MPs as a way of proving its claim to political correctness beyond doubt, so that it can pursue anti-woman policies and beat up on single mothers and teachers and nurses with impunity'.[26]

Unequal Opportunities

Melissa Benn seems to support this view of an anti-feminist sentiment running through the Labour Party's mainstream, arguing that though much has been made of Tony Blair as, like President Clinton, 'one of the first of the baby boomers', there is nothing concrete about these men's association or interest in feminism: 'Instead, their professionally competent, high-earning, glamorously young wives have been offered to us as a sort of substitute: here is my position on female strength and independence! Voter, I *married* her! Like President Clinton, the cultural importance of Tony Blair lies as much in his wife, and young attractive family, as it does in him.'[27]

'First Ladies', as the partners of prime ministers and presidents are inevitably dubbed, are harder to read in a feminist context than are their spouses. While both Hillary Clinton and Cherie Blair have on many occasions played the dutiful wife, they are both famous for having powerful professional positions and are as often dubbed feminist icons as they are denounced as gender traitors. Both have represented women-positive issues whilst being in the public eye, but both are careful to avoid any associations with 'militant' feminism. Whether Cherie and Hillary need Tony and Bill in the long term is hard to say, but Tony and Bill certainly need them.

In common with so many others, these women represent the wholeness of family life and values and the completeness of their husbands, whatever the breadth of their individual achievements and their own ideological perspective. Like the majority of working women they are expected to remain subordinate to the professional lives of their men when it comes to the crunch. Hillary Clinton, in the lead up to the Monica Lewinsky affair, denied that she would mindlessly 'stand by her man', yet – so far – she has, even though her own political future suggests interesting developments following the announcement that she will run for senate. All leaders and prospective leaders reap the benefits of a biddable partner and it is said that Ffion Jenkins, wife of Tory leader William Hague, is being groomed for more public appearances, having managed to remain out of the limelight to date (although the Conservative Party website features a picture of the couple). If they have a child I suspect that her presence at key events will become compulsory.

In the world beyond political rhetoric, although women would do well to retain hope and offer gestures of support for the 121 women in parliament,[28] not much is likely to change in the near future. If anything, it is at the level of rhetoric that most damage is currently being done, since in the last few years more and more studies claim that women have 'arrived' – at least in the world of work. As mentioned in Chapter Three, the key assertion is that the workplace has been 'feminised', which somehow conjures up images of chintz sofas and fresh flowers on every desk. This term has several implications, but in general it indicates that the nature of employment is changing from heavy industry to the communication and service industries, where women are already concentrated. In addition, permanent 'jobs for life' are on the wane, being replaced by more part-time work and temporary casualised contracts. Feminised work, therefore, doesn't have much appeal for women any more than it does for men, but it adds fuel to the argument that women are wholly responsible for these shifting employment patterns. Politically this creates a potential antipathy between male and female workers, raising the old spectre of the dispossessed breadwinner and crediting feminism with huge transformative power, rather than identifying the real 'villains' – the huge multinationals who can shift location swiftly across the globe to wherever labour is cheap.

At the opening of the new millennium, the material position of women is actually depressingly consistent. According to the Equal Opportunities Commission's 1999 annual report, women still earn on average 80 per cent of men's pay,[29] and still face a high measure of sex discrimination in the workplace. One high-profile equal-pay row underlined the ways in which women's work might be distinguished from men's – the case of the protest at Wimbledon in 1999. During this tournament women players argued that they should receive the same prize money as men, and that the practice of awarding prizes according to gendered scales was a historical anachronism. In tennis at the moment only the US Open awards equal money, and Wimbledon's defence was to claim that women should receive less money because spectators prefer to see men's tennis. Carrying these arguments further, and in a ludicrous parody of the equal pay for equal work equation, some commentators and male players argued that men deserve greater remuneration because they normally play five sets compared to women's three.

Moving on to the world of popular music, it was recently claimed that the three female members of the band Steps earn half of what the two male members make. If this is the case, it will, as Libby Brooks observes, 'be slim comfort to Faye, Claire and Lisa from Steps that their predicament mirrors the lives of millions of other women in Britain and across the world.'[30] In the realms of laddish TV, the female stars of the comedy *Men Behaving Badly*, Leslie Ash and Caroline Quentin, complained a few years ago that they were inexplicably paid a much lower rate than the male stars although they were arguably as important to the show.

More obviously machismo jobs do not give up these associations lightly and when it looks as if a woman will prove that she can do the job equally well and hence explode the gendered aspects of the work, men are likely to resort to dirty tactics. Cristina Sanchez, Spain's only top-level woman matador, abandoned her ten-year career in 1999. Regardless of one's feelings about this particular profession, Sanchez's case is an interesting study in how differing arguments are summoned, ranging from that of biology (her breasts got in the way and she wasn't tall enough) to pure illogic (a good bullfighter should be gored, but she managed to fight 60 times in 1998 without injury).[31] Ironically, but unsurprisingly, the only sphere where women's pay consistently outstrips men's is in the realms of heterosexual pornography.[32]

All over the world men are able to sidestep the rhetoric of equal opportunity in order to shore up the most male bastions against the intrusion of women. Rachel Anderson, the only female football agent in the UK, has recently taken the PFA (Professional Footballer's Association) to court for refusing her access to their annual dinner on the grounds that all women, even players' partners, were banned.[33] If it is this hard getting into an association dinner the mind boggles at what one must do to get into the association itself or one of the major clubs.

Another growing trend in the British workplace is the culture of longer and longer working hours and the establishment of shifts which pay no heed to the demands of family life. This culture was recently successfully challenged by Annette Cowley, who won her sex discrimination case against South African Airways claiming that the practice of using double shifts to cover other staff absences affected her ability to care for her daughter.[34] Although this victory may establish a precedent, I wonder whether it will cause any sea-change in male working practices; whether it will be acknowledged that men working long hours also has a knock-on effect on their social and family life.

Since the establishment of the Equal Opportunities Commission, feminist focus on the sexual division of labour has waned and the old feminist arguments on wages for housework have long gone, if recently revisited by Germaine Greer in *The Whole Woman*. Although feminists still lament the fact that housework and childcare have no value and there is therefore no incentive for women to continue doing them any more than men wish to, there has been little movement in gender relations on the domestic front, even though there are a few more 'house-husbands' in evidence. In the early days many felt that a wages-for-housework campaign would condemn women to be associated with domesticity anyway, but men's relationship to this work has changed so insignificantly that it may be time to renew the debates on how housework, childcare and caring are to be given social if not economic value. As Franks says, 'In a market system where unpaid work is invisible, there is no incentive for men to change their identity to encompass low-status, financially worthless activity,'[35] and this 'informal' area of work has yet to be effectively addressed from within the political mainstream.

New Labour is supportive of the proposal to launch the idea of parental leave, which will enable parents to take set periods of time off during the first five years of their child's life; but as this leave will be unremunerated, like most of the pronatalist policies in existence, it only suits those who have the money to support themselves and offers no response to the current construction of the world of work. If work is such a feminised place to be these days, it is surely surprising that it doesn't mirror the needs of the majority of men and women more closely. It is right to be suspicious of all claims that women are holding the reins of power, either at work, in parliament or in the domestic 'choices' we make. As Greer observes, 'The old rule probably still holds good; if women are running the front office, power must have taken refuge somewhere else.'[36]

Chapter Six
Men Under Siege

Men, we are told, have it tough too. Media pronouncements give us recurring images of the young adult male trapped in a cycle of depression and dispossession, leading to identity crises and despair. Increasing concern has been expressed for the future of Britain's young men, with the growing incidence of suicide in this age group suggesting that feelings of profound alienation have reached epidemic proportions. The classic 'explanation' offered is that changes in women's lives and aspirations over the past thirty years have offered new identities for women, but precious little for men. The price of female self-determination and steady strides towards formal equality is, it seems, male nihilism. The struggle for gender equality, rather than being pictured as a pair of scales, is more like a see-saw: if women go up, men must hit rock bottom.

In some cases, a Darwinian response suggests that women have broken away from nature and, in turning away from their instincts, have upset the fine evolutionary balance of the supposedly differing impulses which drive men and women to reproduce themselves. Lionel Tiger in particular argues that with women increasingly in control of their reproductive capacities, men suffer feelings of purposelessness and run away from family responsibility.[1] So feminism and female empowerment become associated with male decline – even at times responsible for it – in a failure to envisage a state of affairs where women can further their own achievements without damaging those of men. But there are two separate issues at stake here and it is unhelpful to find them constantly expressed as one idea.

First there is the question of whether men are suffering an identity crisis in the fallout out from feminism. This could be regarded as a potentially healthy response; a recognition that a change in the lives of women would necessitate a change in the lives of men, as well as what being a man might mean. Sheila Rowbotham foresaw this in 1972 when she asserted that 'the creation of a new woman of necessity demands the creation of a new man'.[2] In truth, most contemporary commentators view the possibility of such change in entirely negative terms, regarding the creation of a new woman as draining away some of the life-affirming energies of masculinity and maleness. There is, at heart, a fear of loss of power which becomes obscured and interpreted as a fear of loss of certainty. Or rather, the two are necessarily intertwined: those most happy with their existing identity are obviously going to be loudest in their rebuttal of change. Many men may just be angry, recalcitrant and willing to defy women's claims to self-definition, but many others recognise that change is essential as part of an overall modernising view of culture, and that therefore participation in these aims will be fruitful.

The second question is whether feminist social critiques and any resultant social shifts are responsible for the material problems facing young men and boys today. Unpopular and/or marginalised perspectives are always going to become the scapegoat for wider ills as a means of forestalling change. One has simply to create a moral panic around certain features of modern life to implant a sense of anxiety in people's minds. Yet if we can look beyond the hysterical pronouncements about the consequences of feminism upon men's lives, we might discover that young men *and* women have every right to feel gloomy about their futures for reasons that have nothing to do with sexual revolution. In a world where work is becoming scarcer and more casualised and yet taking up more and more hours of the day no one profits but those who, to use an old Marxist term, own or control the means of production – often faceless individuals heading up sprawling multinationals. This situation is, ironically, at odds with the presumed material success of 'lads' in the popular magazines. But women's and men's relationship to work is traditionally assumed to be quite different, and so therefore is their experience of unemployment. As Suzanne Franks wryly observes, 'non-working men are feckless and trouble. Non-working women are mothers.'[3] Work *is* man's identity if we think of the ways in which the breadwinning role has developed historically, so unemployment or anxiety about employment threaten their sense of self.

These traditional ordering principles are demonstrated in the film *The Full Monty* (1997), where the lead characters, on finding themselves on the dole and unable to find work for which they are skilled (as steelworkers), declare that they are dinosaurs. As the film progresses, it is clear that unemployment is portrayed as causing wider dispossession, not simply money problems. Each character comes to manifest this dispossession in different ways; one fights against the characterisation of himself as a feckless father as he attempts to keep up his maintenance payments and contact with his son; another suffers impotence; yet another continues to go out each morning as if to work because he can't face telling his wife that he has failed as a breadwinner.

These representations suggest that work makes men complete and this is enforced early on in the film with the sense that Sheffield, denuded of its steel industry, has become a city of women and female dominance – best exemplified by their enjoyment of male nudity in the form of Chippendale-style acts. These men's entrance into the 'feminine' world of striptease will ironically reinstate their position as wage earners and therefore full men – emphasised by the closing shot which tantalisingly promises, but does not deliver, 'the full monty'.

For Franks, the film offers a convincing representation of the long-term prospect of unemployment, asserting that 'It is difficult to overestimate the devastation that unemployment causes for the majority of men who experience it'.[4] *Brassed Off* (1996) offers a more politicised analysis of the effects of unemployment in its depiction of a group of Yorkshire miners fighting the imminent closure of their pit. At the film's climax the colliery band-leader Danny (Pete Postlethwaite) refuses to accept the trophy they win at the national brass-band finals and instead delivers a speech which squarely places the blame on the (then Conservative) government and its investment in market forces over and above any concern for the fates of dispossessed individuals and communities. Danny gets an audience, unlike the women in the film whose efforts to defend the mining community are shown to be futile. The closing credits list the number of pit closures since 1984 and consequent job losses to the tune of 'Land of Hope and Glory'.

It is true that feminists have long sought to change the gendered dynamics of the workplace so that women can realise their ambitions professionally and personally, but this has not created the current economic balance of power. Instead of blaming the women's movement for questioning the sexual division of labour in the first place, one could equally turn to the major political parties, who still implicitly structure policies around the archetypal male breadwinner whom neither they nor 'market forces' can support.

Contemporary society has become a more difficult place for men as well as women to live in, where fewer can expect the reassurance of a job for life. The gulf between the rich and poor has grown and there is an ever more desperate scramble for the plum jobs. Young people, no longer buoyed up by the assurance of a future with a secure job and a living wage, are more likely to drop out, suffer stress, or inflict pain on themselves. Older men and women in a market still unofficially ageist will find job loss harder to cope with, and the future, with a pension plummeting in real value as the entire population ages, is bleak. Perhaps if we were to invest more time in re-envisaging how the world of work operates instead of looking for scapegoats, we could devise fairer and progressive structures which interact better with the dynamics of a changing global economy.

Identity Crisis

I have already articulated how the logic of the backlash is maintained by identifying social ills and foisting them onto the shoulders of bad old feminists. But if we attempt to see past this, what we assuredly find is a highly technologised world and a shifting economy with which people in their ordinary lives, expectations and attitudes have trouble keeping up. In a world where dominant images of machismo and masculinity are still fostered among boys and young men, but where they cannot find release in the acquisition of power, it is not surprising that all we are left with are empty gestures of dominance in 'laddish' behaviour and, arguably, a renewed hostility to any manifestation of female self-determination. But the retreat into laddism isn't purely about the will to power; it also conveys a sense of the boy who never grew up, thereby abdicating any sense of responsibility. This may take away some of the pain and it certainly allows the celebration of the present (as opposed to any sensible investment in the future) conventionally associated with youth. It also enlists sympathy for male shortcomings, even entrenching a sense of the naturalness of certain demonstrations of incompetence. Rather than concentrate on the qualities which have typically been seen to signify masculine strength and dominance over feminine passivity and nurturance, the focus is on 'charming' examples of helplessness and bewilderment. The messages that such images send to young boys are surely damaging. It is arguable that by perpetuating myths about their own incompetence, men are contributing to the identity crises of future generations.

Although much of twenty-first-century living may be beyond our control, we still have choices to make within our personal arrangements and domestic settings, our work and our future. The boyish, incompetent model of masculinity does nothing to help us think about how we relate to each other at the most local level – that of the private sphere. As we have seen, the 'new man' of the eighties was a confusing hotchpotch of ideas, and there are currently no really convincing role models for men that enable them to explore what might be the most appropriate response to feminism, particularly in the domestic sphere, although some pro-feminist men's movements have given much attention to this question. Perhaps the proliferation of retro-sexist images adds fuel to some people's hopes that all this talk of transformation might just be a storm in a teacup.

Nevertheless, one of the logical consequences of feminist lobbying is that men should take on a more significant role in the home. Underlining this is the view that gender differences are largely an effect of nurture rather than nature, and that when it comes to servicing the needs of his children, therefore, a father could actually substitute for the mother. So far, feminists have not had to confront the logical conclusions of this proposition, since the majority of men have not taken up the mantle of chief carer. It does, however, raise interesting questions about how far women are willing to relinquish the dominant mothering role and how the roles of 'mother' and 'father', which in connotations are worlds apart, might finally be collapsed into the egalitarian role of 'parent' with more than simply linguistic appeal.

Rosalind Coward confesses in *Our Treacherous Hearts* (1992), 'I too had intended to share parenting equally. But the intention didn't stand a chance when challenged by something far more primitive and complex – the sense, perhaps for the first time in one's life, that it was *you* who was needed, and that you could do it well.'[5] Coward returns us to the notion of some kind of primal urge governing the need of the mother to assert herself as primary carer; yet how different male and female responses to their children are, setting cultural considerations aside, is never going to be easy to gauge. It may be the case that some women embrace the opportunity to feel 'needed' as an antidote to the alienating effects of the workplace.

Some 'new' men who have tried their hand at house husbandry also seem keen to suggest that they bring to the role an intact sense of their own masculinity. Pete May, though undoubtedly tongue-in-cheek to some extent, insists that 'Dads do things differently,'[6] going on to list his eschewal of nursery rhymes for football chants and love of buggy racing, and concluding that 'carrying a baby turns you into a babe magnet. Overnight.'[7]

The feminist utopia was that corresponding to women's move out into the public sphere, men would contribute more fully to the private. It would be wrong not to concede that something has gone awry in this process. Despite the buoyant reports about women's successes in the world of work, equal opportunities problems are still a part of its daily fabric. To succeed, women can't quite be 'themselves'; and that seems to apply to the experiences of men in the home. The reframing of the world of work and the acceptance that domestic labour *is* work could perhaps encourage real shifts in our association of gender with roles, but the working environment seems to prove more resistant to calls for flexibility by feminists and today's tough work ethic militates against solutions such as job-sharing and flexi-time.

Men in Movement

Feminists have responded to the notion of men in crisis with a mixture of glee, self-satisfaction and concern; at the other end of the spectrum there are grim confirmations that this is what you get for messing with the natural order. Julie Burchill is suspicious of the hysteria accompanying news that (white) boys are dropping behind girls in educational achievement, arguing that 'if boys are to be contenders again, they will get there by feeling oppressed and becoming determined, disciplined and self-reliant, as both girls and ethnic minority children have had to before them'.[8]

For men concerned about the impact they believe feminism has had, the situation is acute. David Thomas's *Not Guilty* (1993) – its title in itself wholly suggestive of his response to feminist critiques – declares that hostility to men is counter-productive and misguided; indeed 'the fact is, people are in pain. And right now, the ones who wear trousers and stand up to piss don't seem to count for much when it comes to being healed.'[9] In a by-now-familiar appropriation of old-style feminist tactics, Thomas recuperates the role of victim for men, implying, bizarrely, that white, middle-class men like him are now on the margins since 'western society is obsessed with women to the point of mass neurosis'.[10] Virginia Woolf made a similar point in *A Room of One's Own* (1929),[11] but in her case it was to underline the irony that while there were countless studies made of women (by men), this did nothing to alleviate their social and material invisibility.

Typically, any contemporary focus on women's issues is interpreted as vehement separatism: or worse, another example of the means by which women's malaise is being addressed and foregrounded at the expense of men. Needless to say, this undermines the impact of feminist critiques at a fundamental level, since feminist observations come to be regarded as evidence of further attempts to colonise the space of discussion and silence newly marginalised male voices. The prevalence of this assumption should not be underestimated, and in all areas of our professional, political and cultural lives there is a sense that many 'women's issues' are greeted with exasperation, incredulity and hostility.

Organisations such as the UK Men's Movement (founded in 1994 and now amalgamated with DADs – Dads After Divorce), echoing feminist backlashers such as Christine Sommers and Katie Roiphe, claim that 'the radical feminists have obtained influence beyond that which their number would suggest they should have, and they have been immensely successful at obtaining their unjust and unreasonable objectives.'[12] They assert that their movement is in contact with other like-minded organisations across the world, and that they have developed as a response to feminist proselytising, representing their actions as part of a male rearguard defence. They portray themselves as offering a family-centred approach which is opposed strongly to what they term 'sexual apartheid' – including any designated women-only space or event (such as car-park spaces and swimming sessions) on the grounds that similar services are not available to men and so constitute sexual inequality. They want women to pay the price for wanting 'equality' by arguing it through to the letter, regardless of the fact that men and women usually have different access to differing levels of power. In the above examples, the women-only events are there to reassure women about safety, as a response to women's self-consciousness about their bodies, or, in the case of the swimming sessions, to comply with religious and/or cultural beliefs. Such events and services have often been set up by local authorities in recognition that our current social arrangements treat men and women differently. If this is to be described as 'sexual apartheid', it hardly needs to be pointed out that it is in fact a response to more deeply entrenched inequalities.

Where positive discrimination has been experimented with (as in the now-defunct Labour all-women shortlists), it is undertaken in recognition that, in environments where custom invites us to expect a male, women are hugely disadvantaged because of their gender. The drive to make largely female appointments in such a context is to allow people to become accustomed to associating these roles with both men and women and therefore to facilitate the path to greater equality. Again, it has everything to do with raising levels of consciousness, and nothing to do with any lack of skill or merit. The UK Men's Movement makes its position on equal opportunities exceedingly clear, taking the term as literally as it can; Suzanne Franks asserts that 'their stated intention is to undermine the [Equal Opportunities] Commission and bring about its abolition, partly by overwhelming the system with complaints from men'.[13] Certainly their website declares 'that the EOC is the most sexist organisation in Britain today'.[14]

If its website offers a representative picture of their work, the UK Men's Movement appears to be comprised of the kind of individuals who, when confronted with women's studies as an academic discipline, want to know where 'men's studies' is – in other words they are missing a rather large intellectual point. In this vein they also object to a Minister for Women and unequal pension entitlements (although not a murmur about the fact that women on average earn only 75–80 per cent of men's pay). It doesn't take too much reading between the lines to guess that the men have been galvanised into action by quite specific experiences. The prime movers have, perhaps, been directly affected by a messy divorce, child custody difficulties and all the financial and psychological damage that can accompany these; yet it can hardly be argued that feminists are directly responsible for this, or that feminists have had a dominant voice in bodies such as the CSA (Child Support Agency), or the British legal system as a whole.

Many of the issues raised by various men's movements are feminist ones too – for instance that men may suffer from lack of choice in their adult role by the fact that their primary identity is supposed to be realised through work rather than their family. In this equation women also clearly suffer because of the association of childcare and domestic responsibilities with their essential selves. Feminists have tried to show how structural ideological inequalities overlay these oppositions and complicate matters – not least, to repeat, the conception that a man without work is unemployed, a woman with a family without work is a housewife. To effect possible transferability between roles, you need to alter the consciousness of those who make these associations. Such a transformation of consciousness might make it easier to convince employers that greater flexibility serves a useful purpose, but should also prompt a revolution of unimaginable proportions in the domestic sphere.

Feminists are looking forward; many of their ideas have to rely upon the envisaging of a utopia which cannot be fully predicted until we are nearer to formal equality. The men's movement, conversely, seems to favour some kind of stasis, or rather a backward-looking return to the sixties, since they are repeatedly citing changes over the last thirty years as the cause of their ills (a period obviously associated with the rise of second-wave feminism). For groups such as the UK Men's Movement, fatherhood and masculinity are essences of a human nature which is static and unchanging, especially in the personal sphere of emotions. While attacking women for having more power today than men, they are really also attacking women for overstepping the mark and not keeping their part of nature's bargain.

Many commentators have pointed out how masculinity relies for its maintenance and definition on what it is not – femininity; if that is being dismantled by women, how do men frame their own difference? It is the possible consequences to our ideas of masculinity as much as the material effects of women's increased entry into the workplace which clearly alarm such men. Women have made some gains and these men want to get even – which means that they want to return to a system of naturalised social inequity. To make this happen they will play the equality card, using feminism's own rhetoric against it and exploiting the fact that the language of equal opportunities cannot assure 'fair play' at all times. Needless to say, male-only institutions and occasions still abound and men continue to find outlets for their own culturally acceptable forms of separatism whenever they can. To argue that men should be offered formal men-only opportunities to even out the 'prejudice' is a sickeningly disingenuous reading of the way our culture is currently arranged along gender lines.

A 'manifesto' purporting to be from the UK Men's Movement which I found tucked within the pages of a book on masculinity in a Midlands university library states as one of its aims 'a fair living wage for every working man...so giving women the freedom to bring up a family at home'; another, more localised, aim was for 'A men's officer in every university to counsel men who suffer feminist harassment by university staff and to provide support in cases of false allegations of rape.' It would be wrong to imply that such perspectives or organisations are necessarily widespread and there have been other men's groups, individuals and journals (such as *Achilles Heel*) who are supportive of feminism and recognise the implications of feminist politics for men too. Yet the view of the UK Men's Movement is one echoed in various forms in the mass media and supported by journalists such as David Thomas, whose argument achieves true bizarreness when he appears to claim that leading political figures are oppressed by their own will to power:

> The undoubted strength and privilege that some men have in the public world should not blind one to the fact that their private selves may be very much less privileged. For example, just think of George Bush. Here is a man whose career reads like a litany of patriarchal power. He's been the American ambassador to China. He's run the CIA. He's been Vice-President and President of the United States. But ask yourself this: would you really want to be George Bush? Does his life seem like an epitome of human fulfilment?... I'm prepared to bet that even George Bush doesn't know who he is any more.[15]

It is interesting how a world created in the image of the privileged white Western man with his interests to the fore should be seen as the force which simultaneously alienates him.

The point that Thomas wants to make is that patriarchal power is complex in its composition (something that feminists have been outlining for some years) and that men, because of their lack of emotional development and the fact that they have internalised feminist demonised images of men, are disadvantaged – he goes as far as to assert that 'men's public power is matched by private disadvantage'.[16] The hugeness of this claim hardly deserves a response, except perhaps to note that the suggestion that the male psyche is damaged and in need of repair all too easily implies that women should stick around to make it better. Unfortunately some of Thomas's book, in common with Neil Lyndon's *No More Sex Wars*, is a reductive kind of me-tooism which trots out a list of ills (women get battered? So do men ...) setting up the terms of human atrocities and human suffering as a new twist on the battle of the sexes.

For Richard Collier, writing in *Achilles Heel* in 1992, anti-sexist politics 'are part of a long tradition of writing by women and men which has sought to question constructions of fatherhood, male sexuality, authority, economic power and so on'.[17] For those who get their pro-feminist radical male politics from *Achilles Heel* the 'new man' might exist in the sense of being a man who has examined his relationship to gender politics and interrogated his own relationship to the hierarchy of power. What marks such men out as so crucially different from the UK Men's Movement or right-wing groups like the US Promise Keepers is that they approach fatherhood, male sexuality and so forth as *constructions* – as roles which may emanate from certain biological givens but which are negotiable in their enactment and in their relationship to motherhood and female sexuality. Such men recognise that power relationships and social relationships could be arranged otherwise and they also acknowledge that power realistically resides in the main with white males.

Just as the UK Men's Movement seems to be harking back to a calmer period in the history of the family prior to the rise of second-wave feminism, the US Promise Keepers want a return to the old systems of family life, but with a difference: they will undertake to perform the role of father and breadwinner effectively and non-violently in return for obedience and co-operation from their wives. In 1991 the US Promise Keepers had their first massed conference in the University of Colorado basketball arena, with 4200 men in attendance. Six years later, on 4 October 1997, thousands massed at the Mall in Washington DC. The frequent choice of sports stadia as venues seems to capitalise on the association of sport with 'male' culture of an exclusive kind, and it seems likely that this connection colours the promises they elect to make. They eventually hope to set up a global ministry with affiliations in the UK, Australia, Canada, South Africa and Germany, and, as a right-wing Christian men's movement, offer another slant on modern men's links to feminism and women's issues.

Although their website is ambiguous about their views on the role of women, citing scripture which seems to embrace notional equality, critics are clear about their actual attitudes. One of the seven promises (Promise 4), that 'A Promise Keeper is committed to building strong marriages and families through love, protection and biblical values,'[18] suggests a simple adherence to tradition and a commitment to 'family values' as understood by the right. The US National Organisation for Women (NOW) has mustered a sustained response, arguing that the Promise Keepers are politically motivated (contrary to their own claims in their publicity material) and are aiming to reassert control rather than participation in the home, as well as being explicitly racist and homophobic.[19]

The only clearly identifiable pro-feminist groups seem to be those which are left-wing in their politics. Even the apparently apolitical US Iron John movement, conceived by Robert Bly and inspired by his book of the same name (published in 1990), seems, in common with the Promise Keepers, to want to awaken the dormant male leader in entirely reactionary terms. Unlike the Promise Keepers, however, this movement is not afraid to stir up a little aggression in the process of getting men back in touch with their authentic primal selves and rejecting being the milk-sops that Bly feels modern men have become. Some of these feelings are arguably revisited in the controversial film *Fight Club* (1999) which depicts men alienated by their corporate jobs trying to reclaim their identities by joining underground fight clubs organised by the anarchic Tyler Durden (Brad Pitt). The director David Fincher summarises the story in disarmingly technological, dehumanised terms: 'It's about someone who says, "I followed my pre-programming, I've opened my desktop, and it's not for me, I need something else – I'm looking for some other specific software that will make me feel alive." '[20]

Men in Pain

Some men under siege are creating barricades to 'protect' their territory. In doing so they are also assigning them new levels of significance. In the case of football, this is marked by a creeping obsession well beyond the sports-dedicated media, into comedy and light entertainment.

No one sport in Britain creates such a safe masculine haven as soccer – paralleled by baseball in the United States – and football celebrity and trivia are now emerging in many different contexts. The activities of boning up on arcane and minute facts about one's favourite team and celebrity is no longer a completely nerdish activity consigned to fanzines and pub talk, but is elevated to the stuff of contemporary history, where facts and figures can be rearranged and picked over to produce an endless array of interpretations. More than that, as I go on to discuss with reference to Nick Hornby's writings, football can tell you about your life.

Women's entry to these domains in any capacity (other than cleaning the kit in washing powder ads) has been slow and difficult. There are women's teams with national and international competitions of their own, although coverage and attendance is problematic in this country. Interestingly, in the USA, where soccer is distinctly unpopular with the massed male sporting audience, women are shaping it in their own image, becoming formidable competitors on the international stage. Meanwhile in Britain, women aren't welcomed into the hallowed halls of professional men's football, as the last chapter's example shows. When Karren Brady became Managing Director of Birmingham City Football Club the keenest interest was in her youth, attractiveness and potential romantic associations with footballers; the fact that she is still in business and successful is something for feminists to celebrate. On the other hand, men's personal lives are irrelevant unless their sexual activity is under criminal investigation, they are gay, or they are dating a female celebrity – to the point that in the past certain misdemeanours have been indulged in order to preserve the flowering of their talent, George Best being a case in point. More recently some celebrities have encountered public censure and issues such as violence against women have received a wider airing because of newspaper reports about Paul Gascoigne and Stan Collymore, in which even the tabloids expressed their disgust.

There is tension within football about the treatment of misdemeanours, particularly in the highly publicised instances of footballers found drunk before big matches or taking drugs, yet some commentators would argue that male culture and in particular the culture around high-profile competitive sports promotes a certain forum where laddish behaviour and violence is endorsed. Within many traditionally male sports, aggression is obviously rewarded. Mariah Burton Nelson, writing primarily about US sporting culture, asserts a clear link between the nurture of aggression in sporting males and a predominance of violence against women:

By creating a world where masculinity is equated with violence, where male bonding is based on the illusion of male supremacy, and where all the visible women are cheerleaders, manly sports set the stage for violence against women. When we begin to understand how male coaches and players speak and think about women and masculinity, it ceases to be surprising that college football and basketball players gang-rape women in numbers equalled only by fraternity brothers.[21]

For Nelson, certain sports shape male athletes' and fans' perceptions of women to the point where routine objectification and abuse of women is entirely naturalised: indeed the sporting temperament itself becomes the justification of such abuse and its defence if criminal proceedings should result.

Nelson further argues that sexual feelings towards women are intensified as a means of deflecting the homoerotic potential of male competitive sport: 'Female cheerleaders, topless dancers, and swimsuit models reassure men that their true lustful feelings are properly channelled not toward the men whose heroic actions and sculpted bodies so excite them, but toward women, or caricatures of women.'[22] If this is the case, it may also explain the marked homophobia still present in most contemporary sport.

Sports culture arguably offers us the most well-defined model of masculinity today, and men's magazines have picked up on these definitions and emphasised them through style and 'health' issues. Femininity is reinstated as a binary opposite, and the possibility of sinking into feminised behaviour, of 'playing like a girl', is one tool used to galvanise men into more aggressive behaviour.

Rosalind Coward is one commentator who thinks that feminists are ignoring the fact that the situation for men has changed massively. She argues that 'feminism had come into being to attack a world of male privilege, a world where the economy was driven by male work and where individual homes mirrored this economic reality. In the 1980s this ceased to be true in any simple sense; the sexual composition of the workforce changed out of all recognition.'[23] But does the so-called 'feminisation of the economy' lead to a feminist economy? Coward offers numerous statistics on this and on the incidence of violent crime and unemployment as they affect men. Statistics, even if you are a social analyst, are hard to interpret as cold data, but Coward uses them as 'evidence' to claim that gender is no longer such an important social marker; rather that one needs to scrutinise a range of inequalities – a complex amalgam of gender, race, class, growing inequality, poverty and wealth – to make sense of our world. Gender is, of course, not the only or the most important variable to measure disadvantage; it does, however, allow one to analyse the condition of women in global as well as national terms in order to recognise that the ideology of femininity, which can operate in different terms, has similar effects across the world. The feminist attack on male privilege may have coalesced with a period of shifting economic certainties, but one cannot help noticing that feminist attacks on other areas – such as the domestic sphere – have yielded next to nothing.

Where I disagree most with Coward is in her suggestion that there has been a sea-change in the way men and men's bodies have been represented. There have in recent years been some highly publicised complaints by men about advertisements which they regard as demeaning to their sex, and Coward agrees, saying that there is now a preponderance of negative images of men in advertising, portraying them as hopeless or as sexual objects for the female gaze. She cites the example of the 1998 Coca-Cola advert, insisting that 'sexual humiliation by women is now a standard part of advertising's rhetoric'.[24] It is true that there are more advertisements of this kind, paralleled by a steady stream of sexually objectified or homely stereotyped images of women and this has as much to do with marketing tactics as it does with changing gender roles; but I cannot see them as equally offensive or noxious because they don't seem to translate into other areas of social experience in the way the equivalent images of the female do. Even some of the most grotesque examples of male objectification – for example, the subjection of pathetically prone males to the ordeal of body waxing on *The Girlie Show* – do nothing to affect our perceptions of these men as people, or prompt us to question their fitness for work, their sexual propriety or anything else.

This is not to deny the complexity or unpleasantness of the underlying message in some cases, but let us not forget that these images, both male and female, are being made, in general, by the same figures in an industry dominated by men. The perpetuation of the image of men as hopeless, henpecked or sexually dominated has the same effect as those images of sloppiness and incompetence favoured by the men's magazines and programmes like *Men Behaving Badly*. This use of irony may suggest a deep-seated anxiety about the future of men in a fast-changing world (and I share Coward's concern about the destiny of young boys and their relative failure to progress in schools), but it is also a plea to be allowed to stay the same.

Coward argues that Nick Hornby and lit-lads of his ilk who have established their careers to some extent on their portrayal of masculinity as inadequacy, suggest that 'parodic self-reflexivity'[25] is an indicator of the changes in attitudes to masculine behaviour. It is moot to consider whether there was ever a time when the construction of masculinity was a simple matter, but it is certainly modish to present it as an obsessional state, the obsessions substituting for emotional fluency. I have already suggested that men suffer from a dearth of revisionary male role models, and Hornby in his writings seems to confront this problem. If we take the example of *Fever Pitch* (1992), Hornby offers us a narrative of his boyhood self confronting the problems of separated parents and absent/long-distance dads.

In the wake of moral panics about the expanding number of single-parent families and the effect this has on boys (most of these families being headed up by mothers), literature of this kind shows us male bonding of the father–son variety, which itself contributes to the boy's identity crisis in growing up. This most particular concern about fathers, I think, also reflects underlying anxieties among middle-aged men about how to find a model of masculinity which incorporates the duties of fatherhood. No one seems to want to repeat the tendency to emotional distance and repression of our forefathers, and men pondering fatherhood or having just become fathers recognise what mothers face too; an inevitable re-evaluation of one's own parents' part in your developing self. Parenting brings home to people the extent to which the world conspires to make boys and girls grow up different, and it is impossible to confront this fact without a certain unease.

Hornby uses the image of his father to investigate his own developing sense of masculinity and of being cast adrift by the emotional distance often found between men and boys which leaves them foundering as they grow up. He vividly describes the means by which the child attempts to present a self acceptable to the milieu around him; how a middle-class lad metamorphoses into soccer fan on the terraces despite fear of derision and abuse. Such writing is fascinating because it adopts a style long favoured in feminist writing and that is the mode of the confessional and fictional autobiography. Women writers have regularly committed their growing pains to paper and there are more manuals on motherhood than you can shake a stick at, but emotionally honest accounts of straight male rites of passage and father–son relationships are still relatively scarce.

Hornby's first-person account is a highly evocative depiction of growing up which also shows how emotional turmoil becomes displaced into some other activity or thing – in this case the father and son's ritual of going to watch Arsenal. Perhaps writings such as Hornby's offer some purchase on male crisis in their attempts to investigate their own contradictions and inadequacies and, as long as it doesn't descend into a self-indulgent reverie about male ways of coping set against female, it can be very positive indeed.

Hornby's conviction that 'the way the game is consumed seems to offer all sorts of information about our society and culture'[26] has some echoes in feminist approaches to popular culture, where something like a Page 3 pin-up will be used as a point of departure for wider discussions about the way women are represented in our culture. He points out the possible consequences of the increase in corporate block booking. This, he hints, creates a greater chasm between the old-style fan-base and those who come to see the top teams regardless of questions of loyalty and support. The gulf is also necessarily one of money, which undermines the other mythology of football – that it is a profession in which any highly talented working-class lad can make his fortune. They still can, but now more than ever it is at the expense of their brothers, just as in the laddism of TV and sports celebrities we see a parodic and nostalgic echo of the working-class hero of the sixties and seventies enacted for the spectatorial pleasure of a middle-class audience.

Susan Faludi's recent lengthy exploration of men in crisis, *Stiffed*, identifies one of the key sources of this crisis in the widespread failure of fathers to offer any nurturance to growing boys, either through absence or through a failure to instil any positive role models around male identity. New Left radicalism of the 1960s is itself portrayed by Faludi as an angry rebellion against the figure of paternal authority, and post-World War Two masculinity is described as being riven with anxieties about what men's proper social roles now are. Faludi argues that there has been a key shift in the representation of masculinity, achieved by the insertion of men into 'ornamental culture'[27] – in other words, they too are now represented in magazines and advertisements as objects to be consumed. Yet she is clear that 'just because men have wound up in the beauty-contest world doesn't mean women have put them there',[28] even though she gives little account of how this state of affairs came about.

Faludi declares that the man in crisis must confront his own reflection – that is, the way masculinity is defined and portrayed in the public arena. Since this public arena is so often governed by men themselves, it is a fundamentally difficult process. Men will have to realise their own part in creating roles and identities which many find alienating. Masculinity is not a ready made suit that you can put on or take off at will and perhaps the way is to stop using traditional 'masculinity' as an aspiration altogether.

However, I do agree that modern man is in crisis and this raises many questions about identity and social role, but the response *has* to amount to more than simply laying the blame on feminism. All contemporary men's movements are taking part in this process of reassessment – even though one might be sceptical about some of their observations – in that they are forced to reflect upon what 'being a man' means. Sadly, few take up the challenge to reinvent themselves or enter the 'private sphere' in more meaningful ways, thus forcing a re-evaluation of men's relationship to work, parenting, sexuality and women in general. Unfortunately, 'men in crisis' fall into the easy trap of blaming women's growing 'advantages' as the cause of their malaise: this satisfies nobody and turns us away from a more politicised recognition that changing employment structures are gradually crippling us all and fatally skewing our relationship to ourselves and each other. While young men and boys reflect on what it means to be a man leafing through the pages of *Loaded* and their female counterparts learn all about men from the likes of *Mizz*, *Sugar*, then *Cosmopolitan*, traditional notions of masculinity and femininity will continue to hold sway, and the 'battle of the sexes' is simply given a contemporary flavour.

Chapter Seven
The Bridget Jones Effect

While men are in crisis, many women continue to flick through the glossies and self-help manuals in an attempt to find their own problems, their own complex identities, reflected there. If some male commentators are suggesting that women, in their will to power, have taken a little bit of men's essential selves with them, women are recognising that 'having it all' demands some complex navigation between what is seen as masculine and what is seen as feminine.

The world of work and public life is so steeped in its masculine image and language that it is difficult for women not to become infected, and as a result be perceived as unhealthily 'masculine' for simply trying to do their work as well as a man. This conflict is echoed out in the film *Working Girl* (1988), where Sigourney Weaver's ruthless and competitive management style is set against Melanie Griffiths' softer reconciliation between her drive for professional recognition and her sexually alluring style of dress — an antidote to the shoulder-padded 'power-dressing' of the early eighties. In fact, this 'unsisterly' conflict is played out as an unseemly battle over the one glittering prize that indicates you've really 'arrived' — getting the man.

Good men are hard to find, if the common-sense aphorisms

of popular culture are to be believed; in fact any available men seem to be in short supply. Belief in this 'fact' shapes the agenda for women's magazines. Having a career is all well and good, but not if it is at the expense of finding Mr Right. All warn implicitly that the heady days of youth, glamour and social freedom are all too soon replaced by the lengthy twilight of terminal single status.

The 'singleton' is, perhaps, the elder sister of the ladette. Once the 'snogging and shagging' of the early years are over and she has reached a certain level in her career, the biological imperative to 'nest' takes over. It is only then that the singleton realises her success in other fields has been at the expense of the one thing that 'really' matters – finding a man. The singleton par excellence is, of course, Bridget Jones.

Bridget Jones's Diary (1996) is one of those books which is credited with catching the mood of the period in its story of a young woman and her friends negotiating the obstacles of contemporary heterosexual courtship. Bridget neatly expresses the tensions of a woman who recognises the rhetoric of feminism and empowerment, but isn't always able to relate this to her fulsome desire for a hero from a Jane Austen novel. The book revives the belief that a good romance thrives on conflict and antagonism between the sexes – all engendered by misunderstandings about the various modes of courtship adopted by each party. Helen Fielding's use of an Austenesque plot dynamic affirms that this 'truth' was known by Jane Austen when she wrote *Pride and Prejudice*. As Aminatta Forna observes, 'It is now assumed that unequal relationships between men and women are the result of biology,'[1] an idea which is supported by TV series such as *Men Don't Iron*, aired on Channel 4 in 1998. Even if people don't really believe that relationships are governed by some intrinsic Darwinian logic, increasing weight is given to the notion that man and woman simply think and express their emotions differently, and the popularity of John Gray's *Men Are from Mars, Women Are from Venus* (1993) is testament to this.

The *Diary* addresses the perspective of gender by affirming that men are different, if equal, and that to 'survive' (in other words to conform and enter heterosexual monogamous bliss) one must learn to speak their language whilst celebrating the peculiarities of one's own sex. In the case of women these include the overwhelming desire for coupledom based on a *Cosmopolitan* view of single womanhood, sexuality and sacrifice.

The second crucial lesson is that 'after all, there is nothing so unattractive to a man as strident feminism.'[2] *Bridget Jones* might be seen as a 'post-feminist' text in the sense that feminist values are situated as somewhere in the past or as an uneasy conscience to a woman who finds the newspeak of 'biological' accounts of sexual difference more comforting.

Fielding, in common with contemporaries such as Kathy Lette, uses the confessional mode of address to encourage the reader to identify with Bridget's vulnerabilities. But in doing so, the reader also becomes complicit in the view of feminism as too prudish, judgemental and unattractive. In her first meeting with Mark Darcy, Bridget claims to be reading Susan Faludi's *Backlash*, but is actually ploughing through *Men Are from Mars, Women Are from Venus*, suggesting that while the former will give her intellectual credibility (a ploy which backfires because Mark Darcy has read it), the latter will give her the pragmatic advice by which to survive singledom.

Kathy Lette, in *Foetal Attraction* (1993) and *Mad Cows* (1997), creates in her heroine, Madeline Wolfe, a figure who also celebrates her frailties and is in many ways a cross between Bridget Jones and Isadora Wing in Erica Jong's *Fear of Flying* (1974). Her relationship with a charismatic TV presenter ends with pregnancy and the prospect of single motherhood, and yet for all her strength of character, verve and humour, Madeline only seems able to carve out her destiny in relation to men. Within this overall plot there is the sense that this is a character with a knowing relationship to feminist arguments, but who casts them as essentially flawed because she cannot get them to gel with her own heterosexual desire. All these books articulate this tension; and in many ways it must be accepted that feminism is popularly perceived as incompatible with heterosexuality because of the tough choices it might be seen to present once one 'politicises' one's own relationships.

As a flawed character Bridget Jones is engaging and certainly many readers' responses are those of empathy and recognition of their own feelings; more than this she is contemporary womanhood packaged and polished by the women's glossies such as *Cosmopolitan*. What glossies are good at, after all, is the stimulation of desire for what we haven't got and the creation of anxiety about our own attributes; they wish us to believe that our aspirations are attainable with a little judicious remodelling and investment in the kinds of commodities advertised within their pages. It is clear that *Bridget Jones* readers are not simply dupes, yet these images are still popularly held to bear some relationship to reality, and insofar as we continue to think that, they do. *Bridget Jones's Diary* offers us a humorous send-up of the means by which we internalise style and trend doctrines, but it does not offer us a way out of them – its irony is unmistakable, but the novel also allows us to identify with Bridget and celebrate our failings in a rather complacent act of self-indulgence.

As Bridget gets her Darcy at the end of the book, we are not only given a narrative with some structural similarities to Jane Austen's work, but some of its dominant values as well. Bridget has made a good match in material and moral terms and will be seen to have learnt the lessons not only of centuries of romantic fiction but also of women's magazines. As Bridget Jones says herself, 'I am a child of *Cosmopolitan* culture, have been traumatised by supermodels and too many quizzes and know that neither my personality nor my body is up to it if left to its own devices.'[3] Fielding's comic irony does not deflect from the fact that readers find fragments of themselves in Bridget Jones to the point where the BBC in 1998 staged a Bridget Jones night devoted to the 'singleton'.

The novel, in common with *Sleepless in Seattle* (1993) and other modern romantic comedies, displays under its comic layer a generation of single women desperate to find a life partner to the point of utter self-abnegation. *Sleepless in Seattle* reinforces the truism that a good man is hard to find, since its heroine Annie Reed (played by Meg Ryan) has to fly from East to West Coast to find hers. It mythologises the idea of knowing one's true love at first meeting by showing her unable to make do with her 'safe' choice of man, who is emphatically nice but decidedly unerotic. The women in this film are portrayed as desperate to pick up the last available men before it's too late, hanging on to safe choices to guard against singledom. Sam Baldwin (played by Tom Hanks) has recently been widowed and is therefore represented as rich pickings, receiving hundreds of letters from women all over America after his son broadcasts his singleness over national radio.

The singleton not only appears in literature, magazines and film but has recently enjoyed huge success on the television, as the popularity of *Ally McBeal* and *Sex in the City* demonstrates. Interestingly, the transatlantic success of these series and of 'singleton' literature seems to indicate that this image crosses cultural boundaries more easily than that of the lad. Both *Ally McBeal* and *Sex in the City* focus on the lives of single professional women and both clearly indicate that the primary ambition of these women is to realise themselves through a meaningful and lasting relationship. In both series, female power is celebrated through the depiction of professional success, but this is often undercut by showing the same women spinning out of control emotionally.

The chief protagonist of *Sex in the City* writes a raunchy gossip-style column about the sexual mores and relationship problems of young New Yorkers. She and her close female friends are represented on one hand as children of the sexual revolution, able to fulfil their desires without censure; yet all their sexual adventures lead them in pursuit of more permanent relationships, and at times implicitly suggest that through sex one can subordinate oneself to male desires and in doing so catch a partner.

Ally McBeal is a successful lawyer who has to come to terms with working with her ex-lover and childhood sweetheart, Billy, now married to another colleague – leading to many *Sleepless in Seattle*-style speculations about whether there is only one true love for everyone. Ally is portrayed as being in pursuit of perfection in her romantic life and in this quest is variously characterised as childlike, naive and neurotic, often accused of being mentally unstable by her friends and colleagues. Regarded by many as a 'post-feminist' comedy – with all the negative connotations attached to that term – Ally speaks the language of female empowerment and choice, but is dogged by insecurities about her own capabilities and in particular her capacity to find the right partner.

The *Bridget Jones* echoes are obvious here, and the frank evaluation of Ally's frailties make for easy audience identi-fication. Yet the series style, which includes 'fantasy' elements mixed in with the realism, allows for the visual depiction of what in fictional terms would be an interior monologue. These moments foreground Ally's silent resistance to sexist put-downs, express her sexual desires and bring to life her subconscious fears (in the first series she is pursued by a spear-chucking baby). Perhaps in a world where women's real needs and motivations are silenced or marginalised, fantasy seems like a viable option.

While the caseload of Ally's company becomes more and more bizarre, often taking examples of sexual and other discrimination to the point of the surreal, the programme seems to revel in exploring situations which dramatise the arguments around 'political correctness' and their practice in daily life. The show's conservative traits have provoked many critiques, but some of these elements are then readily incorporated into the drama – for example, comments about the lead actor Calista Flockhart's weight and the shortness of her skirts. For this reason alone the series is compelling and infuriating, always seeming to reinvent itself by responding to the criticism it gets and always deflecting from the relevance of the issues it deals with by the insertion of fantasy interludes – which occasionally seem to contain a more 'serious' message in miniature.

Sex and the Single Girl

Bridget Jones and its ilk paint a bleak picture of the contemporary singles scene, with women seeking control through the dutiful accounting of the days 'sins' – calorie intake, cigarettes, alcohol. What is most depressing about the 'Bridget Jones effect' is that because people find echoes of their own struggles with femininity in it, it somehow legitimates the measuring of one's own inadequacies through the body. Its messages are as contradictory and conservative as those expressed far more earnestly in Helen Gurley Brown's bestselling *Sex and the Single Girl*, published in 1962 when she was 40, three years after her own marriage to the movie producer David Brown. The book stayed on the bestseller list for seven months from July 1962 and earned her the biggest movie rights sum ever paid out for a non-fiction work at the time.

Sex and the Single Girl is an early example of the self-help manual; written in the first person, its opening sentences are triumphalist in tone: 'I married for the first time at thirty-seven. I got the man I wanted. It *could* be construed as something of a miracle considering how old *I* was and how eligible *he* was.'[4] She continues that 'For seventeen years I worked hard to become the kind of woman who might interest him. And when he finally walked into my life I was just worldly enough, relaxed enough, financially secure enough (for I also worked hard at my job) and adorned with enough glitter to attract him.'[5] Yet Brown insists that her book is 'not a study on how to get married but how to stay single – in superlative style'.[6]

This suggests, rightly, that Brown is full of contradictions: while directing the energies of the single 'girl' towards her future married state, she criticises the stigma attached to the spinster image, rejecting any sense that a single girl's career is merely temporary and claiming for her full adult status (but remaining a 'girl' all the same), both in social and sexual terms. Interestingly the essential accessory for a successful single girl is a room of one's own – 'roommates are for sorority girls',[7] – but this must be coupled with fashion sense, a good body and a good job.

With chapter headings such as 'The Availables: The Men in Your Life' and 'Where to Meet Them', it is not possible to ignore the central purpose of this manual, but her forthright opinions on single female sexuality, and her suspension of any moral judgements on affairs with married men make the book both controversial for its time and highly compatible with the early stirrings of the so–called 'sexual revolution'. None the less, while Brown is cheerfully unromantic and realistic in the expectations she believes her readers should have about their ideal man, she clearly identifies the value and presence of such an ideal, suggesting that success follows hard work and dedication. For Brown, as in her 'baby' *Cosmopolitan*, which she edited in the US from 1965 to 1997, sexuality is the route to female empowerment, so that 'a single woman who doesn't deny her body regularly and often to get what she wants, i.e. married or more equitable treatment from her boyfriend, is an idiot.'[8]

To be sexually powerful, the lot of the successful single girl is self-sacrifice, so that self-discipline in matters of diet, exercise, social networking, interior design and fashion are all equally important. This of course is the self-discipline that Bridget Jones so notoriously lacks. But one thing Brown implicitly makes clear from the start is that femininity has nothing to do with nature and everything to do with artifice – the sexy single girl is the one who invents herself through sheer hard work alone. Brown is testimony to her own philosophy: in 1993 aged 71 she boasted, 'my measurements are exactly the same as they were when I was 17.'[9] Like *Cosmopolitan*, Brown's book is aspirational and as much about class mobility as it is about sexual relations. In this sense, Brown appears more 'enlightened' than the character of Bridget Jones, who lurches from one media trend to another.

Magazine Woman and the Soft Sell

The missing link between *Sex and the Single Girl* and nineties new/post-feminism lies in the rise and rise of *Cosmopolitan* as one of the most influential women's glossies of the past three decades. In its pages the rhetoric of control, choice and empowerment through the female body are rehearsed ad infinitum. But as Susan J. Douglas observes, despite all the flaws of Brown's single girl, she was at the time 'a new kind of role model, and while she was highly convenient to men (and to advertisers), she also opened up new possibilities for women. For once women started thinking that they should be equal in the bedroom, after a while they started thinking they should be equal in other venues as well.'[10] Brown herself is, of course, one of those extraordinary women who prove the exception rather than the rule and whose legacy via *Cosmopolitan* is tangibly felt in the lives of contemporary women, perhaps more than they feel the intellectual legacy of feminism's second wave.

Women's magazines by no means give us an accurate picture of the lives of real women today, but they do tell us much about the dominant female consumer as envisaged by such organs. The Social Affairs Unit's survey, 'The British Woman Today – A Qualitative Survey of Images in Women's Magazines',[11] in its title alone demonstrates a conflation of the image with the real. 'Magazine Woman', according to the survey, is someone obsessed with sex, objectifying men and totally oriented towards selfish satisfaction of her own desires. These traits can clearly be identified in the world of glossy women's monthlies, but to focus on the pure aspirational image as if it in any way reflects the lives of those who read its pages is to ignore the fact that these magazines rely on *making* women feel they have to change. That is their stock in trade. Linda Grant identified the gap in understanding between what was real and what was aspiration in the findings of the Social Affairs Unit, recognising that their assumptions about what *should* be the fodder of magazines provide a telling indication of their preferred model of the ideal modern woman.

Grant emphasises the fantasy role of women's magazines, arguing that, 'underlying every women's magazine is the notion that this publication represents in some way or other an indulgence, an escape; it is the moment in the day which women have to themselves, whether in the 15 minutes while the gratin is browning or standing at the school gates before the hordes are ejected. A women's magazine is the place women have to themselves. It represents their dreams and their aspirations.'[12] Perhaps her evocation of what women's magazines represent is itself too innocent of their broader agendas and links to real and carefully researched consumption habits, but this view of why women read magazines accords with some ethnographic research on why women read romantic novels and may certainly be how individual readers justify their own 'habit' to themselves.[13]

Women's reading practices are far more complex than the survey suggests; we are aware that magazines are in the business of trend-spotting, or reinventing the 'new' in order to keep us buying them, and to some extent we see ourselves as knowing and sceptical readers. However, the whole Bridget Jones phenomenon suggests that we are drawn to these images because they remind us of our own deficiencies and simultaneously offer reassurance about our human failings; we are homogenised and individualised within the pages of the same magazine. Just as Bridget Jones's 'real' self is always deferred from emerging until the next orgy of overeating, drinking, or relationship misery is over, so the glossy magazines suggest that we come to them from a position of inauthenticity, but that through them we discover the 'real me'. They therefore play on a sense of lack, the feeling that women 'want' to be themselves but haven't quite got there.

Magazine advertisers have not been immune to the pulls of irony and they often parody the position adopted by women's magazines as if to undercut them – they pretend to reassure the spectator that there is no ideal type of femininity, yet visually they refuse to offer what most would consider to be the full range of female norms in terms of age, colour, size and physical ability. Take, for example, the advert run by Nike in 1994 which showed a group of women, naked but for a kind of loincloth, with one of them holding a baby. The copy read, 'Where is it written that unless you have a body like a beauty queen you're not perfect? You're beautiful just the way you are. Sure, improve yourself, but not in pursuit of an impossible goal. A synthetic illusion painted by the retoucher's brush. Get real. Make your body the best it can be for one person. Yourself. Just do it.' This is an advertisement with no product placement at all – just a picture of women in soft focus, homogeneous body types and white skin tones. In offering a critique of constructions of ideal beauty and the tyranny of the perfect body it addresses the spectator in terms of individual freedoms, using a form of ventriloquism by speaking through a 'feminist' voice – and flattering us by assuring us that we don't really fall for media manipulation. Yet of course while the advertisement *tells* us that we are all different, the image says otherwise.

In a similar vein, in 1999 an advertisement for Vaseline Intensive Care Deodorant showed four young white women in their underwear, smiling. They aren't so much capturing our gaze as deflecting it by laughter. The copy, adopting the exclusive first-person plural favoured by women's magazines, asserts that 'we all know that the idea of the perfect female body is nuts. A fantasy dreamt up by men (usually men with beer bellies)', and in common with the Nike ad it exhorts us to reject the normative aspects of femininity in favour of some kind of self-determination.[14] Whereas Nike characteristically tell us to 'just do it' – a slogan worthy of the 'new' feminists – Vaseline takes us into the realms of the absurd, suggesting that even if we continue to be dissatisfied with most parts of our body, at least we can be proud of our armpits. In fact the advertisement's movement from the lead copy's third-person plural ('They hate their boobs, their bums, their knees and their noses. They love their armpits') to the collective 'we' underneath the photo suggests a masculine viewpoint which yet again positions these women as objects to be looked at.

The importance of all of this is that women are being confronted with images which they knowingly acknowledge as unreal ideals, but which link into wider cultural beliefs about body image and which, by their very ubiquity, reinforce those beliefs. Such messages are contradictory, so it is not surprising to see young women identifying with fictional characters like Bridget Jones who diet on one hand and yet attempt 'feminist' resistance on the other.

In the February 1994 edition of *Elle*, there were two features on the schoolgirl look, one of which explained that 'the look has taken the two polar opposites of sexual fantasy – the schoolgirl and the slut – and produced a style that is positive and invigorating. Saucy stereotypes have been plundered for their most evocative elements...'[15] This supposedly playful use of provocative images is further explained in another piece in the same magazine which has inset photos of Twiggy and Cilla Black as they were in the sixties, set against contemporary models wearing retro sixties outfits and adopting similar simpering poses. We are encouraged to accept that the image set in the nineties is utterly different in its connotation, because the models in question are self-consciously playing with the 'girly' look. Unfortunately the image itself offers the same echoes of mock innocence, vulnerability, the air of being looked at. An instinctive response is 'what's the difference?'

The text tells us that the nineties image is somehow different from the sixties one in that it denies the 'patriarchal' role in constructing it. Lamentably, as in so many instances in women's glossies, the 'post-feminist' image amounts to a reclamation of a pre-feminist image. Any objections we might feel are set up as contradictory because we are supposed to 'know' that this is ironic and therefore not exploitative.

You'll Never Be Miss World...

The reason the 'schoolgirl' got more than the usual attention lavished on a passing fashion phase was because it foregrounded the preference for waiflike models, with its unpleasant connotations of a fixation on the young pubescent body, and prompted widespread criticism that such images contributed to the epidemic of eating disorders among young women. Since the glossies are always thirsty for new 'trends', girliness comes and goes, but there has been a persistent interest in the retro, making it clear that there is an anxiety about how women can or should be portrayed.

During 1996 there was a brief flirtation with an even more banal image from the past: 'cute, groovy and more than a touch retro, the happy housewife look swings into style.'[16] Here, the housewife label suggests a slightly more mature female image, but the term 'happy housewife' strikes the oddest chord – not since Betty Friedan talked of the 'Problem that has no name' in *The Feminine Mystique* (1963) did these two words sit easily together. What is especially striking is the baldness of the caption, which stands intact without irony – has post-feminism reached the stage where its own 'playfulness' is deemed self-evident?

In another glossy during the same year, a feature on Dutch supermodel Karen Mulder had her posing with a variety of household items; she is reported to exclaim, 'I just love to clean...I could clean all day as long as I was being

photographed.'[17] The image, while drawing attention to its own
fakery, suggests the impossible fusion of two male fantasies –
that of the ideal domestic labourer with a flawless physique. The
article emphasises that 'as a physical specimen she is almost
perfect: her figure is remarkable, like a finely carved piece of
willow, while her skin, her hair and her eyes appear to have
been created by computer.'[18] Strangely enough, 1999 saw the
development of the first cyber model, Webbie Tookay, created
by Stephan Stahlberg and signed by the Elite model agency,[19]
proving once and for all that the feminine ideal was impossible
to measure oneself against and could only be reliably generated
by technology. Another cyber superbabe, Lara Croft, heroine of
the computer game 'Tomb Raider', goes one step further: her
dimensions are pure male fantasy.

There remains a common tension in the glossies between the
public and private spheres, but generally magazine women are
still exhorted to be good at everything. They tend to ignore the
domestic in terms of labour, on the grounds that their implied
aspirational reader has better things to do; but the elision of the
domestic space with a working woman's 'free time' means that
domestic labour becomes conflated with 'leisure'. Yet although
housewifery has just about been made sexy, mothers, despite
Demi Moore's appearance, pregnant and naked, on the cover of
Vanity Fair in 1991, have not. Celebrities can flaunt their
pregnancies, producing ever more glamorised airbrushed
images of this condition, but in real terms it is still incompatible
with certain forms of female celebrity.

This was further underlined by the deposing of Nicki Lane,
Great Britain's entry for Miss Universe, when it was revealed
that she had had a child at the age of 14.[20] The reasoning behind
this was allegedly a 'no ties' rule because of the travel the
winner has to do. This was not the first time 'scandals' about
single parenthood have surrounded beauty pageants, but given
the contemporary context it might not have been too much to

expect a degree of enlightenment on this front. The 1998 Miss World contest, screened on Channel 5, was supposedly 'modernised' and, unlike Miss Universe, was free from bikini rounds. Instead footage was shown of groups of contestants leaping around on the beach in their bikinis. All that is demonstrated, as Libby Brooks reports, is Channel 5's view 'that assumptions about beauty and a woman's right to capitalise on her physical assets had changed sufficiently to free the contest from the feminist charge of exploitation'.[21] The illusion of feminine purity has to be sustained and, as Yvonne Roberts warns, 'if you somehow inadvertently expose the fact that behind the bikinis and the candy floss, it's still all about sex, baby, then it's out on your butt.'[22]

The rebirth of Miss World on terrestrial TV in 1998 and the announcement that Miss World 1999 was to be staged in Olympia, London, suggests that no feminist victory around the uses to which the female body is put is safe. With magazines like *Cosmopolitan* still market leaders in their field, the women's magazine could do a lot to empower its readers. Yet it tends to resort to the most banal 'post-feminist' rhetoric of empowerment, within which its identity as the vehicle for a particular range of advertisements can remain intact. Such magazines tend to recycle trends and revisit old female ills such as PMT, anorexia, bulimia and more latterly dysmorphia.[23] This term, used to signify hatred of one's body to the point of revulsion, often at one's weight or the shape of one's nose or breasts, might at a lesser level be embraced by many women. *Bridget Jones* is the epitome of body dysmorphia and, as Germaine Greer observes, 'what is truly depressing about the false dawn of feminism is that, as we have been congratulating ourselves on largely imaginary victories BDD [Body Dysmorphic Disorder] has become a global pandemic.'[24]

The white, Western, slim, depilated body may have become a universal aspirational image – one which dominates the mass media – yet what is called a 'disorder' is in many ways a logical response to the demands of patriarchy. As long as women are encouraged to believe that by engaging in rabid consumerism they are articulating a freedom to be 'themselves', this kind of dysmorphia will grow. It is difficult to see what feminism can do in response, since a recognition of such beauty standards and feminine codes of behaviour may well enable women to make strides in their chosen profession, whilst a rejection of such standards – inegalitarian, racist, sizeist and ageist as they are – is greeted with a howl of post-feminist ironic laughter.

Naomi Wolf is just one commentator in a line of many feminists since the 1960s who have recognised the tyrannies of the beauty industry and the pain it can inflict on women. In *The Beauty Myth* (1990), she states her amazement that 'the rightness and permanence of "beauty's" caste system is taken for granted by people who study quantum physics, ethnology, civil rights law; who are atheists, who are sceptical of TV news, who don't believe that the Earth was created in seven days. It's believed uncritically as an article of faith.'[25] Her 'solution' is less carefully worked through than her account of the problem, in that change is perceived as coming necessarily through women, despite her acknowledgement that the rewards and punishments for subscribing to or rejecting the beauty myth are generally in the hands of men. Wolf, who in her later book *Fire with Fire* (1993) submitted that 'at the end of the twentieth century – at least in the First World – populations are not controlled mainly by laws and militias, but by images and attitudes',[26] tends to be reductive in her manifestos for change. In her anxiety not to blame men for sexism and inequality, the 'enemy' becomes a strange creature indeed.

Wake Up and Smell the Testosterone

Obviously women's magazines and their conservatism cannot be held responsible for the 'failures' of feminism, but they are in part guilty of recognising that being a woman is a 'problem', then identifying the problem as one requiring therapy or self-help: 'women are repeatedly told that their problems can only be dealt with through individual, rather than collective, responsibility... women's magazines are so structured, ideologically and formally, that they cannot offer political resolutions to what they consistently define as "personal" problems.'[27]

The magazines, in common with *Sex and the Single Girl*, fragment any sense of commonality between women in favour of representing women as always in competition for scarce resources – men, jobs and beauty. While feminists were trying to liberate women by encouraging them to stop seeing themselves in relation to men, women's glossies took their lessons from Helen Gurley Brown and portrayed the snaring of men as woman's primary aim in life. The language of courtship never became much more sophisticated than this, and women were re-educated to abnegate their own identities whenever it came into conflict with that of their partner. They were encouraged to return to a false consciousness, flying in the face of feminist discussion about self-determination, to believe that the only way to find their true selves, motivations and desires was in the pages of their monthly magazine.

Of course this paints an unnecessarily two-dimensional picture of magazine woman, because she is and isn't a part of all women's lives. However, *Bridget Jones* became a bestseller because women recognised within its irony their own experiences of popular culture, and especially the tensions between the lure of feminist politics and the fear of losing one's femininity. This perception of the incompatibility of feminism with having a meaningful heterosexual relationship has unfortunately been perpetuated beyond reason to its current status as self-evident 'truth'.

One of the main problems at the moment is the paucity of straightforward feminist comment within the media. Since feminism has become the 'f-word', and therefore doesn't sell, magazines, TV and radio are reluctant to give it much space. Committed 'feminist' television is a long way from commercial realisation, and in Britain feminist magazines have not yet offered a plausible alternative to their glossier sisters. The most famous one, *Spare Rib*, expired in 1993 and *Everywoman* passed away not long after. Its successor, *Sibyl* (launched in March 1998), was hanging by a financial thread in 1999, relying as it does on regular subscriptions, donations and sales in the odd alternative bookshop. In the USA, *Ms* magazine was founded in 1972, relaunched in 1990 without advertising and ceased publication in September 1998, relaunching again in March 1999 to the cry of 'We're Back! Wake up and smell the Estrogen' [sic]. Saved in part by its original founder, feminist icon Gloria Steinem, who gathered a group of women investors to buy it,[28] the return of *Ms* suggests that feminist magazines are still in demand and can still reach a wider audience, but only just. Whether in the long term it can endure as a magazine without advertisements in a world where they are the defining identity of mainstream magazines is a difficult question.

The one period during which *Cosmopolitan* attempted to become a more worthy publication, it suffered a significant dip in sales and soon returned to its tried and tested formula of skirting round the more serious or self-conscious questions of female identity. Like the other big glossies, *Cosmopolitan* is a complex site of negotiations around what it means to be 'post-feminist' – as Esther Sonnet and I have said elsewhere, 'what the mainstream glossies are out to sell is a feminine power which can be located in both the escapist and pragmatic elements of the magazine; and this particular notion of "power" seems to reside in the female body and the female heterosexual response.'[29]

Bridget and her friends are also seeking empowerment within the terms of their own singleton status; and there are some well-chosen moments of female anger at male inadequacy, as when Bridget's friend Sharon rants: 'In years ahead...There won't be any men leaving their families and post-menopausal wives for young mistresses, or trying to chat women up by showing off in a patronising way about all the other women throwing themselves at them, or trying to have sex with women without any niceness or commitment, because the young mistresses and women will just turn round and tell them to sod off. . .'[30]

For Paul Wallace, the entire 'Bridget Jones Effect' is an accident of population imbalance, and he says that the massive sales of *Bridget Jones's Diary* 'owed much to the fact that there were so many of these women around. In 1996, over a quarter of women in their early thirties were single.'[31] Even though this figure does not account for women cohabiting, Wallace claims that this is a much higher proportion than in the recent past, but that a reversal is due because of the declining birth rates in the late 1970s and the fact that 'when birth rates are rising, as they were in the 1950s and early 1960s, there will be more girls born in later years compared with the number of boys in preceding years . . . wind the clock forward and the result is an excess of Darcys and sweet revenge for Bridget Jones.'[32] In case we don't live long enough to see Bridget Jones's revenge, we may have to start rethinking our already complicated relationships to the glossies and ask whether their contribution to our fantasy life is offset by the damage they may do to young women's self-esteem.

Chapter Eight
Old Prejudices, New Exclusions

The 1999 inquiry into the Stephen Lawrence murder identified the Metropolitan Police as rife with 'institutional racism', a term which rapidly achieved mainstream currency and, though not a new concept, offered space for debate. Defining institutional racism allowed for a consideration of both unconscious as well as conscious prejudice and arguably provided a better model for examining the ways in which society perpetuates racism while seeming to implement legal and civic measures for its prevention. The term does indeed act as useful shorthand to account for the ways in which race blindness persists alongside unexamined assumptions about the qualities which underpin diverse ethnic identities. Whether its rapid dissemination within popular cultural circles signifies a new enlightenment, or simply the grasping of a phrase which assuages national guilt without the necessity for any decisive action, remains to be seen. It is clear that the acceptance of the idea that the white majority might be unconsciously racist could itself become the means by which people deny full responsibility for the consequences of their behaviour: anything prefixed with 'institutional' sounds impersonal and difficult to challenge. On the face of it, at least, fixing on this term has led to an extensive review of policing and police training, aimed at addressing the means by which such 'unconscious' prejudices are implanted.

Feminists in the 1970s who demanded a revolution in consciousness were aware that ideas govern our relationship to things in a fundamental way. In today's society we might feel it appropriate, therefore, to identify the dynamics of an institutional sexism which is also part of the fabric of many professions; which informs women's experience of work in general and gives shape to the fabric of their daily lives as inevitably as racism does for people of colour. In this case I suspect that the term would not be so rapidly embraced, since it smacks of the 'political correctness' which new feminists and others wish to avoid at all costs; but also, numerically, women can hardly be cast as a 'minority' in any population, and many are reluctant to countenance the idea that women might be globally marginalised.

The police investigation into the murder of Stephen Lawrence was exposed, through the efforts of his family and friends, as one of dozens of examples of racially motivated injustices which could no longer be covered up. More proactive recruiting strategies to ensure that the racial make-up of the police force reflects the characteristics of the local population may encourage a trickle-down effect, whereby close association with members of other ethnic groups will increase under-standing among whites. But the message for these new black recruits may be that tackling racism is their problem, even though identifying prejudice when it occurs hardly ever makes you any friends.

To offer an account of some omnipotent and overarching racist, sexist or heterosexist force would be to face the accusation that you have the conceptual naiveté of a conspiracy theorist. Moreover, to argue that institutional *sexism* exists and that it still reflects the overall balance of power between men and women would be construed as yet again casting women in the role of the eternal 'victim'. Victims in the present day, having received a 'power feminist' makeover, must pick themselves up, brush themselves off and go and seize some power, rather than whinge about the patriarchy. I suspect that when the guilt has subsided, our black and Asian population will be similarly counselled to 'take control' of their lives by recognising the range of opportunities a fully global culture can offer you.

Institutional racism, sexism and homophobia are all driven deeper by popular cultural habits of either sidelining these issues or making difference the subject of voyeuristic exoticised attention. In terms of the way different groups are portrayed, the situation for white (presumed straight) women is perhaps distinct from black and Asian women and men, and gay men and lesbians. White women suffer from an excess of visibility – our global market is shaped in their image if we are to believe the advertising which so freely exploits their bodies. And whereas black, Asian and other ethnic women are visible to a great extent, it is usually in specific locations or contexts. Rarely are they associated with ideal-type femininity. Black men, out gay men and women are more often than not left invisible, especially when 'normal' life is being portrayed. Often they play roles which enable the perpetuation of stereotypes, or appear in images which entrench their material position as outsider – a 'gay' scene can add a surprise twist to a soap, defy a heterosexist reading of a beer advert, but it doesn't attempt to encourage us to view all depictions as equal.

In every case youth is prized above all, so that in some areas of mass culture, such as magazines, popular music, fashion and lifestyle, older people are almost universally invisible, unless they are Cher or Mick Jagger. Interestingly, though, 'youth' culture seems to be ageing, along with the huge ageing baby boomer generation; but when baby-boomers nostalgically hanker after images of their childhood and early youth they also revitalise the stale old images of imperialism, patriarchy and homophobia undiluted. It is true that many of the cultural productions of the sixties and seventies were themselves rife with contradictions and it is possible to read series such as *Charlie's Angels* as sources of empowerment for the female spectator even while they assuredly provide a retrograde sexual spectacle. The 'three little girls who went to the police academy' have also metamorphosed into formidable women; moreover, they form a 'sisterhood' of protection, as many of the victims they help are women. Susan J. Douglas describes this ambiguity thus: 'it was watching this – women working together to solve a problem and capture, and sometimes kill, really awful sadistic men, while having great hairdos and clothes – that engaged our desire.'[1] Perhaps it is this identification of the retro with the sexy which accounts for the success of films such as the two Austin Powers movies (1997 and 1999). But the new ironists tend to exploit these contradictions only to retain the 'femininity' of the female image – and if an argument can be made that these women are 'in control', like the celebrities who pose for the lad magazines, all well and good. The ironic argument hasn't been pushed so far with regard to race as yet; on the day when *Love Thy Neighbour* (1972–6: a British sitcom based on the exchange of ritualised racist abuse by two men) makes the re-runs, we'll know that things are completely out of control.

Feminists have long argued that images of women are used to sexualise and subordinate them, and the idea that to show a woman is to show her as defined by her body shape, colour, age and compliance with conventions of beauty still has much legitimacy. The white woman is fetishised and prized above all else, and when black, Asian and other ethnic women are presented for our gaze, it is often with an 'exotic' label implicitly tagged on. (This is certainly true of the portrayal of the character Ling in *Ally McBeal*.) In the case of African-American or African-Caribbean women especially, it is often a highly sexualised image, which suggests aggressiveness on the part of the woman as well as sexual voraciousness. I have already discussed the ways in which Mel G's 'scariness' is as much about her perceived racial difference as it is about her strength of personality.

African–American feminist bell hooks argues that such contemporary stereotypes have their origins in the slave experience, contending that 'the shift away from the image of white woman as sinful and sexual to that of white woman as virtuous lady occurred at the same time as mass sexual exploitation of enslaved black women... As American white men idealised white womanhood, they sexually assaulted and brutalised black women.'[2] From here evolve the modern images that privilege a white face and features and, as Patricia Hill Collins observes, preserve a social/sexual hierarchy among womankind: 'judging white women by their physical appearance and attractiveness to men objectifies them. But their white skin and straight hair privilege them in a system in which part of the basic definition of whiteness is a superiority to blackness.'[3] Even when Barbie is marketed in various skin tones, she only really emerges as a white doll in blackface; the aim of course is to widen her appeal to all communities, even though the image of material success she represents often has little relevance.

White female beauty becomes the indicator of desirable womanhood and if white women are unhappy with the way they are objectified, they have to acknowledge that at least the image is able to offer them advantages over the more common negative images of black womanhood as whore or matriarch. It makes visible their ordinary lives and experiences, albeit through a grossly distorting lens. From a British perspective, Annecka Marshall claims that 'the inability of Black women to achieve our socioeconomic and political potentials has been institutionalised by the relegation of Black womanhood as being synonymous with rampant sexuality.'[4] If white women have experienced a sexual division of labour because of the association of female labour with domestic skills and caring, how much more constraining to be associated primarily with sexual availability and servicing. The association of black women with sexual availability in Britain, however, does not mean that black women are presented to us as one of the archetypes of feminine beauty in the fashion and glamour industry, and black women rarely make the covers of glossy magazines.

Race and Visibility

Feminist and anti-racist critiques are not always compatible, and since the emergence of the second wave, there have been tensions between black and white women about whether, in a feminist model of equality, all women are necessarily perceived as equal behind the rhetoric of sisterhood. For white feminists, gendered oppression may appear structurally more fundamental than racist oppression; in the past it was even assumed by some white feminists that, being oppressed themselves, they could not exert a racist authority over other women and men. Some black feminists are keen to preserve this woman-identified perspective within their own anti-racist politics because of a commitment to fighting sexism in their own communities, but as a consequence they have also found themselves reluctantly positioned as adversaries to black men.

For black women, then, the major struggle has been for visibility within both sexual and racial politics and the acknowledgement of a different experience of sexism which makes some of white feminism's fundamental tenets inappropriate for them. To take one obvious instance, the model of family life and its rejection by white feminists had a mixed response from black women, for whom, although the family might remain a central site for the perpetuation of gendered inequalities, it may also be the nucleus of community-wide resistance to racism.

Jenny McLeod, writing about her mother's experience coming to Britain from Jamaica in the fifties, notes some of these contradictions, recounting how 'the feminism of my mother and the women of her generation was born from a knowledge they carried within themselves, something they learnt about at the feet of their own mothers and their mothers before them: racism and inequality.'[5] She points out that the extreme racism which this generation met when they arrived from the West Indies created tensions between men and women where men felt compromised by their inability to find decent work, respect or status and perhaps directed their anger towards women. McLeod's contention is that these difficulties within relationships have persisted into the subsequent generation, where men are finding it difficult to commit to one partner and that 'on the one hand, women see men as a great source of pain and continual disappointment, while on the other, they see them as a vital and necessary ease within their lives.'[6]

There does seem to be a parallel here with black Americans, where popular racist theories about the existence of a 'matriarchy' within black communities, which gained credence during the 1960s via the Moynihan Report, were internalised. Black women were blamed for emasculating their men, even though it was more properly the material effects of a racist economy that employed black women more readily than men, thus often making black women the breadwinners for their family.

From the above it is clear that it is not just white female beauty and physical attributes which are normally privileged, but ways of life and family organisations that reflect the commonality of white experiences. This makes for another form of cultural invisibility, whereby black people are assimilated into the same broad range of behaviours and aspirations or, if they fail to conform, are seen to be 'anti-social' in some way. I am aware in writing this book that so-called lad and girlie culture excludes black men and women to a large extent, in that the most prominent and successful celebrity exponents – the Chris Evans and Denise Van Outens – are white and it is assumed that their opinions and experiences reflect those of their audience. Individual black people may be present and highly visible, as is Mel G (who identifies herself as mixed-race), but their identity may not be a defining issue.

Girl power, because of Mel G's presence, may be influential among young black girls who would recognise the music industry as one of the professions with a relatively high race profile and who might also be drawn to All Saints; but the aspirational model of girl power articulated in the Spice Girls' book of the same name recognises no significant ideological or material barriers for people of colour, focusing on sheer determination to pursue one's dream. Programmes such as *The Girlie Show* return us to an emphatically white gaze, just as laddish television is almost universally white in its cluster of celebrities and references, although programmes such as *They Think It's All Over* have occasionally offered largely predictable responses to black male sportsmen.

Gangsta Culture

I have already observed that there may be a huge gulf between the attractiveness of lager-swilling 'lads' on the street and their fictionalised counterparts on TV and in glossy magazines. Whereas the vulnerabilities of the latter are played up, in the case of the former it is their destructiveness which defines them in the portrayals offered by the popular media. Particularly displayed in the form of football hooligans, these lads are reviled by the same popular press who incite them to xenophobia, homophobia and lecherous sexism in the first place.

In terms of black culture, the men most vilified by the white press are gangsta rappers. This is particularly the case after the recent shooting of the Radio 1 DJ Tim Westwood, believed to be a result of his profession and his association with gangsta rap. However, it is clear that to make this association of gangsta rappers with violent crime is to risk a racist perception of one phenomenon as it reaches the mainstream, set against other aspects of black British youth culture which remain invisible in white-dominated society precisely because they don't invoke the same kind of fear.

It is also telling that it is only black youth who are seen as vulnerable to the criminal undertones perceived in this extraordinarily popular form of music; the hordes of white youths who also buy it are presumably regarded as largely immune. The music itself has wide global appeal across ethnic boundaries, and even its extreme sexism and generally controversial lyrics – particularly the constant references to women as 'bitches' by male rappers – does not stop the emergence of a large female fan-base.

As Helen Kolawole illustrates, the gangsta scene is based on retro values, deriving its style from seventies blaxploitation films such as *Shaft*, and therefore recovering a style statement from an essentially racist origin. Many rappers would see their lyrics as a further rejection of racist value systems and an expression of black disenfranchisement, where marginality is recuperated by celebrating it and refusing to comply. As in the case of white lad culture, the stereotypes of women come through as if skipping the feminist gaze of the past three decades. Additionally and problematically for its exponents, the visual imagery which it borrows also denotes black men 'as gun-toting misogynists who reinforce all the sexual myths and associations of criminality that continue to plague Black men to this day'.[7] The fact that gangsta rap has generated a moral panic here as well as in the United States makes it clear that, although there are many unpleasant aspects of the music in its misogyny and portrayal of violence, it is viewed with caution primarily because it emerges from poor black ghettos.

Some of the men behind gangsta rap are clearly in crisis; it is not simply a question of them not knowing who they are any more, it is a question of finding genuine visibility, acceptance and support in any environment which automatically thinks of black men as potential criminals, and where they are far more likely to be the victim of a violent crime than their white male counterparts. As I have hinted already, and as Helen Kolawole observes, 'gangsta rap has never been much concerned with political correctness,'[8] which sets up tensions between black men and women where confrontation may be avoided to present a united front against racism, or where female rappers may attempt some form of redress by expressing their own views, and rejecting misogyny through their lyrics. At its worst gangsta rap can promote sexism of the most poisonous and retrograde kind, but this should not be allowed to obscure the fact that terms of abuse designed to animalise and sexualise women have a wider currency across cultures and ethnic boundaries and are used to much more devastating effect, albeit with the language suitably toned down, in the mainstream.

Queering the Pitch

There is a danger when isolating a particular group for the purposes of voicing concerns about violence that you imply that violence is peculiar to these groups, or that it emerges purely as a reaction to their conditions of existence. Realistically, glamorised male violence is as much at the heart of 'our' culture as it is a side-effect of dispossession and poverty from 'theirs'. A culture of violence is clearly inherited from centuries of conflict over territory, possessions and greed, but in contemporary terms violence and aggression are often seen as something innate to the male psyche, as well as something to be nurtured in specific contexts. I argued earlier that the macho world of competitive sport fosters a naturalisation of violence in an arena where women become objectified and where aggression is stoked up for the sake of the 'game'.

The dark underside of the nation's love affair with football is its racism, its violence, its sexism and homophobia. Racism in particular has been an enormous problem in professional football and its homophobia has never been better demonstrated than by the fall from grace of Justin Fashanu, who eventually committed suicide. In 1999, an incident between Liverpool's Robbie Fowler and Chelsea's Graeme Le Saux where both were fined for their on-pitch behaviour suggested that homophobia among players is endemic. Fowler taunted Le Saux, after constant on-pitch tensions between them, by offering his backside to him. This incident was picked up hungrily by the national press, whereby we were assured that Le Saux was happily married – an assurance which created a curious ambiguity around press responses to the incident. Was it assumed that we were outraged by Fowler's gesture or more concerned about Le Saux's sexuality?

Girliness and laddishness offer a number of inflections within lesbian culture, particularly since the mid-eighties and the erotic revival of butch and femme identities. Within the mainstream, of course, laddishness and lesbianism would offer a predictable link, providing opportunities to present the lesbian as the mannish woman who in her desire for women is 'aping men'.

Interestingly, though not surprisingly, the mid-nineties' brief flirtation with lesbian chic found the girliness of the 'femme' image appealing and extremely visual. Before the Spice Girls offered us girl power as a catchphrase, lesbian subculture was getting the 'girlie' treatment. In 1993 the now infamous cover of *Vanity Fair* showed Cindy Crawford pretending to give kd lang a 'shave' in a barber's chair. The butch and femme oppositions were played for visual humour rather than to make any serious point about lesbian chic, and this cosmetic overhaul of the dominant image of lesbianism has, needless to say, nothing to do with the ways lesbians might perceive each other, and a great deal to do with heterosexual male fantasy.

Increasing sexual candour in representation gives us the illusion of a tolerance of 'queer' imagery. In reality the majority of such depictions derive equally from a long tradition of depicting lesbian sexuality as the equivalent of heterosexual foreplay. Just as 'new feminism' has become a term to court those women frightened off by old-style radical feminism, so this cosmetic overhaul of lesbian images courts a younger audience who reject traditional lesbian identities. According to Stephanie Theobald, 'gay woman' instead of 'lesbian' is 'what you call yourself in the lonely hearts columns to make yourself sound stripped clean of all politics and reinforcing the fact that you don't hang around droopy breasted at the Michigan Womyn's Music Festival . . .'[9] The lesbian chic image touted in the mainstream press and running like a rash through the British soaps in 1994 has now subsided, although programmes such as *Gaytime TV* have a more glamorous glitzy image than was the case with the more earnest news-oriented *Out* on Channel 4 a few years previously. The contrast between these two shows is interesting in that *Gaytime TV* offers a more 'mainstream' magazine format, featuring numerous straight as well as gay guests. But some might contest that, in common with the 1999 Gay Pride event in London, it has sold out to a rather superficial 'lifestyle' orientation at the expense of the acute political edge which maintained an activist dimension to gay and lesbian issues in the past.

Diva, one of the first glossy wide-circulation magazines for lesbians in this country, is committed to a glamour format, so that its visual style is a cross between that of mainstream women's glossies and the more sexualised lad mags. For Cherry Smyth, 'it's easy to see why glamour has become attractive to lesbians for whom in the mid-eighties it was a sell-out to patriarchy to be "trendy", and collusive with a misogynist fashion industry to wear anything but jeans and baggy jumpers.'[10] What is important about *Diva* is the opportunity it provides to produce images of lesbians over which they have some degree of control. Questions arise, however, about the consequences of producing a lifestyle magazine visually on a par with the mainstream glossies and which by and large operates the same regime of exclusion along the lines of age and size in particular and race to a lesser extent.

Several years on from its launch, *Diva* is none the less a success story. It has moved to monthly publication and consolidated a particular style which has found an advertising base willing to support it and exploit the lavender pound. There is realistically the normal give and take between advertising and features that is found in all women's glossies, whereby advertisers have to believe that their needs are being generally served by the content of the magazine. Its implied readership seems to be young, style-conscious devourers of music, film and alcohol, with a highly energetic nightlife. It particularly appeals to relatively prosperous lesbians and bisexual women who, in an era where our politics are supposed to be our lifestyle, supposedly want nothing more than to be able to consume and be addressed as consumers on a par with straight young women.

What saves *Diva* from the utter vacuity which descends over the majority of women's magazines is the dissemination of gay and lesbian news and the inclusion of serious features embracing a far broader range of health, work and political issues than is at first suggested by the visuals. From my own reading of 1994 editions set against those from the late nineties, the 'serious' content has been markedly slimmed down. However, at the level of representation, it offers a timely appeal to lesbians who want to see themselves reflected favourably. This is also true of the gay male lifestyle magazines in an environment where, apart from sporadic bursts of visibility in mainstream entertainment, the best one can hope for are targeted programmes such as Channel 4's *Queer as Folk* or BBC2's *Gaytime TV*. As Alexander Doty and Ben Gove point out, the range of mass media images of gays and lesbians is still profoundly limiting and often relies on depicting 'gay men as hysterical prissy queens, and lesbians as violent predatory butches'.[11]

Lifestyle Politics?

In a way, gays and lesbians have found that the most positive strategy in recent years has been to develop more 'separatist' realms of interest, including the increasing numbers of bars, clubs and other venues as well as dedicated lifestyle magazines. In the States particularly, the value of the pink pound (largely gay male finance) has enabled some shifts in visibility for gay and lesbian issues, as well as prompting some multi-national companies to recognise their gay and lesbian consumers and target them accordingly. Greater visibility can lead to increased tolerance and with this the power to lobby for important policy shifts. From a radical perspective, however, this partial success owes more to economics – to the recognition of gays and lesbians as a 'market' – than to profound changes in society. It can be no coincidence that political issues in this context become somewhat diluted.

Just as feminists are frequently blamed for preventing straight women from wearing what they want and pursuing greater heterosexual freedoms, so many younger lesbians see the women's movement as prudes who attempt to cramp their style, revile S/M practices, and are pro-censorship in their largely anti-porn stance. Important lesbian critics such as Joan Nestle have attacked the feminist response to butch/femme identity and other manifestations of lesbian sexuality and as a consequence have opened up much wider debates about how lesbian sexuality can be depicted and made visible for other lesbians.[12] It seems, none the less, counterproductive, not to say dangerous, to hold up this rather inaccurate picture of the feminist as oppressor in order to assert that modern lesbians can do without gendered politics.

Glossy black magazines such as *Pride* (which appears to be primarily aimed at women) similarly signal how the African-Caribbean community in Britain have carved out an identity which recognises their exclusion within mainstream glossies, male and female, as well as acknowledging that different 'lifestyle' issues arise from a black British context. The magazine contains all the predictable health, beauty and style features, but its features explore the impact of racism on every aspect of black culture, ranging from the fallout of the Lawrence Inquiry (with an interview with Sir Paul Condon) to prison rape, and the white appropriation of Notting Hill. The latter feature reports on how the likely further gentrification of Notting Hill, in the wake of Richard Curtis's 1999 film of the same name, particularly affects its black residents, who have been experiencing increased marginalisation over the years. The article recalls how the Notting Hill of the fifties 'was like a massive slum'[13] which became the home of many of Britain's African and Caribbean immigrants, and how the multicultural feel of the area is made visible through its carnival in August, which was established after the riots of 1958. Precious Williams suggests that this white gentrification 'emphasises the differences between the new well-heeled professionals and celebrities who are flocking to Notting Hill (mainly white) and those who've lived without luxury or opportunity for decades (predominantly Black)'.[14] The piece pulls no punches about the effect of racism in what was traditionally seen as a black area, and how white trendiness costs many black people their livelihood.

'Separatist' publishing for both black communities and gay and lesbian ones offers opportunities for visibility, the establishment of a wider community through communication and the creation of a black, gay or lesbian aesthetic, freed from the appropriation of a racist and homophobic mainstream. These magazines can operate at varying levels of political savvy, but a measure of their success is also an acknowledgement that in popular culture few avenues have opened up for the portrayal of multicultural or sexual realities. There is, of course, the issue that magazines targeted at particular groups can further marginalise their interests, yet it goes without saying that the negotiation between separate spheres and any renewed challenges to a mainstream which not only fails to represent these constituencies adequately but also causes them suffering, rejection and material hardship is a complex one.

If the simultaneous celebration of and challenge to marginality expresses the condition of black, gay and lesbian relationships to the mainstream at the moment, for white straight women, as I suggested earlier, there is a need to respond to an excess of visibility and an absence of any significant shifts in the approach to representations of women over the past thirty years. In addition, many feminists had long felt that there should be a particular commitment to raising the profile of issues of race, sexuality and ability in the feminist fight against oppression. In the wake of almost wholesale rejection of 'political correctness', the only abiding legacy of 'identity politics' is the feeling that no one has the legitimate right to speak for anyone anymore.

There are problems with identity politics, not least in the awareness that many high-profile speakers may emerge from, or now be a part of a more privileged sector of their group due to educational or economic opportunities. But theoretically, identity politics signifies a commitment to raise the profile of the effects of widespread social oppression and alienation; to reject it out of hand is to accept the view of the happily privileged centre that political correctness is outmoded, ineffectual and plain old dull.

Chapter Nine
They Think It's All Over...

At the dawn of the new millennium much re-evaluation of our past has been taking place, and cultural explanations of gender conflict tussle with 'scientific' ones which give a genetic explanation for almost every aspect of our behaviour, and inscribe a dreamily fatalist edge to human life. Alongside the straightforward biologistic accounts, which often try to suggest that our genetic programming will finally get the better of our will to rise above sex-specific destinies, are the dire warnings of environmental damage which not only affects our health, but in its projected impact on our fertility could dictate new unimaginable shifts in social behaviour. Out of these speculations emerge the trend-watchers, who, based on their observations of the recent past, make predictions about the shape of the future, which inevitably include speculations about women's roles, or predict disaster in the face of women's increased economic independence.

According to Paul Wallace, for example, global demographic shifts during the past 30 years necessitate a change in emphasis on issues of health and work, but will also transform the market place as the majority of consumers age and discover different priorities. His book emphasises the likely shifts in commerce and finance, supposedly aiding the reader to make profitably informed guesses about what kinds of business are likely to be in the ascendant and what kind of assets will increase in value. But some of his specific points about fluctuations in population affect women in particular, because these shifts more than anything declare the consequences of women forging new identities beyond childrearing. He argues that in an environment where there is a new generation of relatively safe and effective contraceptives, it will become more common to have a single child, and more and more women will eschew motherhood altogether. Wallace foresees a potential 'backlash against the modern values that have created the agequake. If ageing and population decline intensify, social panic might break out. At its most extreme, the future could resemble *The Handmaid's Tale*.'[1]

Even though, as Wallace says, there are means to deal with such phenomena which aren't punitive (other countries, such as Sweden, have already experimented with pronatalist policies which reward people for having children), it is clear that a fixation on declining rates of fertility could lead to a greater demonisation of feminism if childbirth were to be equated with social responsibility. In such a context, feminists' adherence to a woman's right to make reproductive choices might seem treasonable.

Wallace's incitement to moral panic might be also interpreted as unapologetically Western in its focus, since populations are still rising exponentially in developing countries and, globally, women's problems are connected to an excess of children rather than a dearth of them. Globally, it is women and children who experience the extremes of poverty in the face of an economy where multinationals seek out the cheapest labour. Of course, for quite different reasons, feminists have been arguing for greater social responsibility towards children for years: they have asked for the incorporation of childbirth and child rearing into their demands for full sexual equality in the public sphere, and a consequent recognition by men of the need for them to take a more active part in childcare.

For feminists the social benefits are clear; more men would recognise the value of such work and outside work patterns could be transformed along child-friendly lines so that men would have greater opportunity to play a part in their children's upbringing. So far all we have in Britain is New Labour's rhetoric of child-friendly government in a decade where all workers regardless of sex are statistically getting to see less and less of their children.

Other trend-gazers apply a more heavy-handed ideological interpretation to their data in an explicit condemnation of the gains of feminism in the Western world. For Francis Fukuyama, writing in *The Great Disruption* (1999), the transformation in gender roles, the drop in fertility and the wider impact of feminism over the last 30 years have contributed to the social disruption of the developing information age. He claims that women are among the chief victims of the 'great disruption' in social values:

> Educated, ambitious and talented women broke down barriers; proved they could succeed at male occupations, and saw their incomes rise; but many of their less educated, less ambitious, and less talented sisters saw the floor collapse under them as they tried to raise children by themselves in low-paying, dead-end jobs or, for the poor, on welfare. Our consciousness of this process has been distorted by the fact that the feminists who talk, write, and shape the public debate about gender issues come almost exclusively out of the former category.[2]

The market shift to service industries which led to more women in the workplace has, according to Fukuyama, created a profoundly individualised, morally corroded society with increased crime and more and more fatherless families.

Although Fukuyama suggests that social disruption needn't be a bad thing because it allows order to be remade, it is clear that women's role in the current disorder is crucial and that therefore in Fukuyama's high-liberal world view, women are the guardians of social order.

No one doubts the crucial role of mothers in the early stages of life, but Fukuyama tries to add weight to his justifications of their special role by making comparisons between human kinship patterns and those of the animal world, to conclude that 'men, in other words, have a biological disposition to be in effect more promiscuous'.[3] None of these arguments are new, but one can only offer the obvious response that our postmodern relationship to nature and the animal kingdom is at the very least genetically modified and comparisons are therefore problematic. Other studies of animals have concluded that females of many species are casually promiscuous and that primates may have a long term mate, but that this does not stop them mating with other males. Either way, these studies tell us far less about female sexuality or male power than we can deduce from observing our own social mores.

Fukuyama's observation that Asian countries such as Japan have not been as adversely affected by the 'great disruption' because of their adherence to family values and the maintenance of the nuclear family is hardly likely to raise a cheer from feminists. Whatever else might be said of his work, its linking of disruption with changing roles for women, and recourse to accounts of primitive human behaviour to justify sexual difference in the twentieth century, amount to woman-blaming of a perniciously infectious kind.

In all of this, woman's role as reproducer of the species comes to the fore and there certainly seems to be a greater interest in motherhood than ever before. If I were a trend-watcher I would certainly be warning women to expect a bombardment of blandishments about their special role in the survival of the human race. Where physical coercion is no longer feasible, women are being emotionally blackmailed by the new/old patriarchs and the backlashers to return to their role as moral guardians of society and the family to the point of utter self-effacement. In this hugely materialist world, who would be willing to act as moral guardian unless the pay is good?

Here we come full circle to some rather elderly second-wave feminist arguments and a single question: if motherhood is so sacred, why isn't it worth anything? Why is it individual women who bear the cost of their own maternal labour if the future of the world depends upon us? Children have less and less contact with adults beyond their parents in a world where families are fragmented. In the Western world women may be bringing up children at a greater cost to themselves because, generally, no extended family exists to bring support, wisdom and friendship to the child. The only response to the likes of Fukuyama is to point out that the family is historically bounded in its changing definitions; children have physical links to their mothers, the importance of which feminists have never denied. Most mothers who work might even like to spend more time with their children; but emotive arguments about biological destiny are hardly relevant in a world where what really divides people are money, economic privileges and educational opportunities. Feminists of the twenty-first century must ensure that they don't start believing all the trend-watching propaganda; that they don't just give up the fight and go shopping.

While women as mothers are making a brief comeback, it is women as sexual beings that retain the most attention in the new/old patriarchy and still provoke the ire of numerous female newspaper columnists. Charlotte Raven accuses 'British feminists' of inertia and failure to mobilise over specific issues: 'A woman's naked form is projected on to the House of Commons. The feminist community's response? No comment, unless you count the conversations which took issue with Gail Porter's celebrity on the basis that her arse was too small.'[4] This outcry is her response to the fact that NOW in the USA have just had a conference on images of women in the media which will hopefully return the issue to a wider sphere. I agree with Raven that this is good news in an environment in which, lately, no one has felt equal to the task of working through the complex maze of questions about the gaze and who is in control of it in order to make some fairly basic declarations about offensiveness. I don't agree with Raven, however, that no British feminist is equal to the task of launching such a critique; it is more a simple fact that there is significantly no organisation of similar breadth and influence to NOW in Britain that can undertake a sustained campaign.

Until the 1990s, NOW never had much appeal for me because of its liberal profile as an organisation mainly involved in lobbying, but in a decade where political inertia has set in, where many people don't seem to know how to organise their beliefs, and where there are fewer forums to debate beliefs seriously, a similar organisation of feminists in the UK might enable young men and women to reassess gender roles and to look forward to a more liberating future for everyone.

My single experience of a women's demonstration in America is of a gathering about violence against women at the Mall in Washington DC in 1995. The demonstration, organised by NOW, drew many thousands of people and combined stalls, music and speeches. What struck me most were the responses of people in the boarding house where I was staying, most of whom (educated, white, middle-aged men and women in the main) felt keen to attend, and none of whom trotted out the usual stereotypes about feminist activists that you would definitely encounter in Britain. Compare this to my last experience of a London demonstration on the same topic which, on a cold day in November in the early nineties, attracted probably two or three hundred women at most and ended with a broken PA system in Trafalgar Square and a desultory rendition of 'I Will Survive'.

When I teach my course on feminism to students, many,

eager to get active, ask me for contacts and are disappointed with what I can offer them. Of course, those interested in political reforms can join the Fawcett Society, which has a facility to set up local small groups but nothing on a par with the numerous NOW chapters to be found all over America.

I still foresee problems with the setting up of what might be regarded as a feminist 'leadership' whose views get a wider airing than those with less access to networks of communication, but I believe that there is a need for women to be able to make contact with each other as part of an organisation that addresses itself in the broadest terms to women's current sexual inequality. The internet throws up many a women's site or feminist zine, which show the resources available for a more collective response to patriarchy and which take advantage of the information age. Such an organisation may essentially have to reconcile itself to being anodyne enough to offer a broad alliance among women, and it should be accessible and applicable to 'ordinary' women, so would also have to learn the lessons of past problems with race blindness, elitism and homophobia. Above all, it must be an organisation of women first. This kind of separatism is hopelessly unfashionable in the present climate (and was never greeted as an attractive option for the majority of women), but is essential if social change is actually going to reflect ideological change. Some men will always resent their exclusion from membership and deduce that this excludes them from the debate (which doesn't and shouldn't necessarily follow), but these are the men who perhaps at heart resent the possibility that a woman might enter the public domain on equal terms. In any case, an internet location would allow easy access for all who were interested in the affairs of such an organisation.

Maybe the establishment of such an organisation is a long way off – such things require commitment, resources, the will of many women for them to happen – yet many of us are wearied by the seemingly endless battle to change people's consciousness. We have to move beyond all the truisms about feminist authoritarianism around personal adornment, which is after all an expression of fear of the unknown and fear that a movement based on gender can only be alienating to men. From my point of view feminism hates not individual men but patriarchy – the manifestation of power, knowledge and consciousness generated in the interests of men, as it is affirmed and perpetuated by individuals who aren't always men and don't always know what they do. Feminists have a responsibility to make it clear how patriarchy works and what sexism (and racism and homophobia) does to women and men, so that people can decide for themselves.

Second-wave feminism 30 years on is the peak of a very long and sometimes bitter struggle to liberate women from oppression, but the terms of that oppression never stay the same and therefore feminism must constantly adapt itself to new environments, and perhaps make new alliances with other groups and political bodies. Moreover, as women make more links across national borders to create a global dimension to feminism, the issues of concern shift in emphasis and broaden in scope. And while the terms of oppression change, the ideological basis of that oppression – patriarchy – remains constant. This is the enduring challenge to feminism. Most young people are familiar with the language of feminism because it has been imported directly into the rhetoric of lifestyle magazines and contemporary politics; indeed some would argue that modern mainstream politics is so dependent on its representation in the mass media that image is everything. In modern politics lifestyle issues are imported to strengthen the message; images of men with their families help inspire our trust, smart clothes make us believe in efficiency and sometimes the dropping of formalities (as when Tony Blair removed his tie at the Kosovan refugee camps) can even suggest compassion. In this light perhaps feminists would profit from a makeover; but being the old spoilsports that we are, we'll probably take great pleasure in anatomising the tyranny of dress!

Given that there is a growing trend to want to be 'politically incorrect' in cultural criticism and serious debate, it is incumbent upon feminists to rehearse the consequences of such a position, no matter how 'uncool' it may be. Freedom of speech as a defence has always been used to best effect by those who have such freedoms in the first place, so feminists can point out that different groups of people have differing degrees of access to the kind of speech which can reach a wide audience. Needless to say, total freedom of speech allows for the abuse and harassment of the disempowered, and for the entrenchment of certain attitudes which gain credence precisely through a freedom of speech which must privilege the powerful. These were the kind of abuses that a notion of political correctness could go some way to alleviating, but now that the whole concept has been subject to misuse, overuse and ribaldry over the last decade, it is important to try to preserve some means by which oppressed groups can respond.

Feminists must also debunk the sense that we inhabit a world which already offers us a range of ready choices and where we can play at sexy vamp with no ill effect because we are 'in control' of the look we create. Lifestyle politics leaves many victims in its wake – those who don't conform to its preferred images and those who are too poor to exercise 'control' over their lives through the 'liberation' of consumerism. With a growing gap between rich and poor, one might argue that there are more victims than ever. To deny that a 'victim culture' exists is to overlook the fact that today's society breeds more losers than it does winners.

For Rosalind Coward, feminism's 'future in the new millennium is to face up to the problems of its success'.[5] What I have tried to assert throughout this book is my belief that feminism's success has been announced rather prematurely, and what we seem to witness at the level of popular culture is, on the one hand, a flourishing of nostalgia for the 'old order' of babes, breasts and uncomplicated relationships, and on the other a sense of powerlessness that as, taken individually, such images are 'harmless' or trivial, so there is no clear platform for critique. For Susan Douglas, nostalgia is not just reactionary but patriarchal: 'for what gets looked back on and celebrated as pathbreaking – James Dean, Elvis, the Beatles – are the boys.'[6] None the less, she also reminds us that growing up female with a mass media that constantly reinvented ways to make women's oppression seem sexy, promoted radical self-consciousness in girls of her generation from an early age. Perhaps young women of this generation will feel similarly galvanised by the current atrophy of political debate; maybe this time someone will feel nostalgic for the heady days of the women's movement.

Bibliography

Ballaster, Ros, Margaret Beetham, Elizabeth Frazer and Sandra Hebron, *Women's Worlds: Ideology, Femininity and the Woman's Magazine*, Macmillan, London, 1991

Barrett, Michèle, *Women's Oppression Today*, Verso, London, 1980

Bayton, Mavis, *Frock Rock: Women Performing Popular Music*, Oxford University Press, Oxford, 1998

Benn, Melissa, *Madonna and Child: Towards a New Politics of Motherhood*, Jonathan Cape, London, 1998

Blake, Andrew (ed.), *Living Through Pop*, Routledge, London, 1999

Bloom, Allan, *The Closing of the American Mind: How Higher Education Failed Democracy and Impoverished the Soul of Today's Student,* Penguin, Harmondsworth, 1987

Bly, Robert, *Iron John: A Book About Men*, Element Books, Dorset, 1991

Bradby, Barbara, 'Freedom, Feeling and Dancing: Madonna's songs traverse girls' talk', in Sara Mills (ed.), *Gendering the Reader*, Harvester Wheatsheaf, Hemel Hempstead, 1994, pp67–95

Brooks, Ann, *Postfeminisms: Feminism, Cultural Theory and Cultural Forms*, Routledge, London, 1997

Brown, Helen Gurley, *Sex and the Single Girl*, Bernard Geis Associates, New York, 1962

Cartmell, Deborah and Imelda Whelehan (eds), *Adaptations: From Text to Screen, Screen to Text*, Routledge, London, 1999

Clark, VéVé, Shirley Nelson Garner, Margaret Higonnet and Ketu H. Katrak (eds), *Antifeminism in the Academy*, Routledge, New York, 1996

Collins, Patricia Hill, *Black Feminist Thought: Knowledge Consciousness, and the Politics of Empowerment*, Routledge, New York, 1991

Coote, Anna, and Beatrix Campbell, *Sweet Freedom: The Struggle for Women's Liberation* (second edn), Basil Blackwell, Oxford, 1987

Coward, Rosalind, *Our Treacherous Hearts: Why Women Let Men Get Their Way*, Faber & Faber, London, 1992

—*Sacred Cows: Is Feminism Relevant to the New Millennium?*, HarperCollins, London, 1999

Davies, Jude, "'It's Like Feminism, But You Don't Have to Burn Your Bra": Girl Power and the Spice Girls' breakthrough 1996–7', in Andrew Blake (ed.), *Living Through Pop*, Routledge, London, 1999

de Beauvoir, Simone, *The Second Sex* (1949), translated and edited by H.M. Parshley, Penguin Books, Harmondsworth, 1972

Denfeld, Rene, *The New Victorians: A Young Woman's Challenge to the Old Feminist Order*, Warner Books, New York, 1996

Dennis, Wendy, *Hot and Bothered: Sex and Love in the Nineties*, Viking Penguin, New York, 1992

Doane, Janice and Devon Hodges, *Nostalgia and Sexual Difference: The Resistance to Contemporary Feminism*, Methuen, London, 1987

Doty, Alexander and Ben Gove, 'Queer Representation in the Mass Media' in Andy Medhurst and Sally R. Munt (eds), *Lesbian and Gay Studies*, Cassell, London, 1997

Douglas, Susan J., *Where the Girls Are: Growing Up Female with the Mass Media*, Time Books, New York, 1995

Echols, Alice, *Daring to be Bad: Radical Feminism in America 1967–1975*, University of Minnesota Press, Minneapolis, 1989

Edwards, Tim, *Men in the Mirror: Men's Fashion, Masculinity and Consumer Society*, Cassell, London, 1997

Ellmann, Mary, *Thinking About Women*, Virago, London, 1979

Faludi, Susan (1991), *Backlash: The Undeclared War Against Women*, Chatto & Windus, London, 1992

—*Stiffed: The Betrayal of the Modern Man*, Chatto & Windus, London, 1999

Fielding, Helen, *Bridget Jones's Diary*, Picador, London, 1996

Franks, Suzanne, *Having None of It: Women, Men and the Future of Work*, Granta Books, London, 1999

Freely, Maureen, *What About Us?: An Open Letter to the Mothers Feminism Forgot*, Bloomsbury Publishing, London, 1996

Fukuyama, Francis, *The Great Disruption: Human Nature and the Reconstitution of Social Order*, Profile Books, London, 1999

Greer, Germaine, *The Female Eunuch* (1970), Paladin, London, 1971

—*The Whole Woman*, Doubleday, London, 1999

Griffin, Gabriele (ed.), *Outwrite: Lesbianism and Popular Culture*, Pluto Press, London, 1993

Gunew, Sneja (ed.), *A Reader in Feminist Knowledge*, Routledge, London, 1991

Hill, Dave, *Men* (Predictions series), Phoenix, London, 1997

Hite, Shere, *The Hite Report: A Nationwide Study of Female Sexuality,* Summit Books, London, 1977

hooks, bell, *Ain't I a Woman: Black Women and Feminism*, Pluto Press, London, 1982

Hornby, Nick, *Fever Pitch,* Victor Gollancz, London, 1992

Jackson, Stevi and Sue Scott (eds), *Feminism and Sexuality: A Reader*, Edinburgh University Press, Edinburgh, 1996

Jarrett-Macauley, Delia (ed.), *Reconstructing Womanhood, Reconstructing Feminism: Writings on Black Women*, Routledge, London, 1996

Koedt, Anne, Levine and A. Rapone (eds), *Radical Feminism*, Quadrangle Books, New York, 1973

Lumby, Catharine, *Bad Girls: The Media, Sex and Feminism in the '90s,* Allen & Unwin, Sydney, 1997

Macdonald, Myra, *Representing Women: Myths of Femininity in the Popular Media*, Edward Arnold, London, 1995

Maynard, Mary and June Purvis (eds), *(Hetero)sexual Politics*, Taylor & Francis, London, 1995

McRobbie, Angela, *Postmodernism and Popular Culture*, Routledge, London, 1994

—'Pecs and Penises: The Meaning of Girlie Culture', *Soundings*, Issue 5, Spring 1997

Medhurst, Andy and Sally R. Munt (eds), *Lesbian and Gay Studies*, Cassell, London, 1997

Morgan, Robin (ed.), *Sisterhood is Powerful: An Anthology of Writings from the Women's Liberation Movement*, Vintage Books, New York, 1970

Nelson, Mariah Burton, *The Stronger Women Get, the More Men Love Football: Sexism and the Culture of Sport*, The Women's Press, London, 1996

Nixon, Sean, *Hard Looks: Masculinities, Spectatorship and Contemporary Consumption*, UCL Press, London, 1996

Oakley, Ann and Juliet Mitchell, *Who's Afraid of Feminism? Seeing Through the Backlash*, Hamish Hamilton, London, 1997

Paglia, Camille, Sex, *Art and American Culture: Essays*, Penguin Books, Harmondsworth, 1993

Phoca, Sophia and Rebecca Wright, *Introducing Postfeminism*, Icon Books, Cambridge, 1999

Pilcher, Jane, *Women in Contemporary Britain: An Introduction*, Routledge, London, 1999

Porter, David (ed.), *Between Men and Feminism*, Routledge, London, 1992

Roberts, Yvonne, *Mad About Women: Can There Ever be Fair Play Between the Sexes?*, Virago, London, 1992

Roiphe, Katie, *The Morning After: Sex, Fear, and Feminism*, Hamish Hamilton, London, 1994

Segal, Lynne, *Straight Sex: The Politics of Pleasure*, Virago, London, 1994

Sommers, Christine Hoff, *Who Stole Feminism?*, Touchstone Books, New York, 1994

Spice Girls, *Girl Power!*, Zone/Chameleon Books, London, 1997

Thomas, David, *Not Guilty: In Defence of Modern Man*, Weidenfeld & Nicolson, London, 1993

Tiger, Lionel, *The Decline of Males*, Golden Books, New York, 1999

Waghorn, Jane (ed.), *A Message for the Media: Young Women Talk*, The Women's Press, London, 1999

Wallace, Paul, *Agequake: Riding the Demographic Rollercoaster Shaking Business, Finance and Our World*, Nicholas Brealey Publishing, London, 1999

Walter, Natasha, *The New Feminism*, Little, Brown, London, 1998

—(ed.), *On the Move: Feminism for a New Generation*, Virago, London, 1999

Wandor, Michelene (ed.), *The Body Politic: Women's Liberation in Britain 1969–1972*, Stage 1, London, 1972

Whelehan, Imelda, *Modern Feminist Thought: From the Second Wave to 'Post-feminism'*, Edinburgh University Press, Edinburgh, 1995

—and Esther Sonnet, '"Freedom From" or "Freedom To"...? Contemporary Identities in Women's Magazines', in Mary Maynard and June Purvis (eds), *(Hetero)sexual Politics*, Taylor & Francis, London, 1995

Wolf, Naomi, *The Beauty Myth*, Chatto & Windus, London, 1990

Fire with Fire, Chatto & Windus, London, 1993

Woolf, Virginia, *A Room of One's Own* (1929), Grafton Books, London, 1977

Notes

Introduction

1   The pageant took place on 7 September 1968. For a brief account of the demonstration, see Alice Echols, *Daring to be Bad: Radical Feminism in America 1967–1975*, University of Minnesota Press, Minneapolis, 1989, pp92–6.

2   A recent example is that of Karen Loughrey, aged 15, who declares in an interview by *Children's Express* that although she cares about feminist issues, 'I wouldn't call myself an activist, I wouldn't go out protesting and saying burn your bras, because I think that's pathetic.' In Natasha Walter (ed.) *On the Move: Feminism for a New Generation*, Virago, London, 1999, p5.

3   Susan J Douglas, *Where the Girls Are: Growing up Female with the Mass Media*, Time Books, New York, 1995, p160.

4   This ad campaign is mentioned by Myra Macdonald in *Representing Women: Myths of Femininity in the Popular Media*, Edward Arnold, London, 1995. She argues that, 'The Wonderbra woman is nevertheless distinctive from Mae West in her ease with her own femininity. Mae West's self-conscious sashay and parodic acting draw attention to her performance as performance, in a way often reminiscent of the drag queen' (p177).

5   Germaine Greer, *The Whole Woman*, Doubleday, London, 1999, p50.

6   *The Sun* published a photograph of Sophie Rhys-Jones, Countess of Wessex, in May 1999, which revealed one of her breasts.

7   Katharine Viner, 'The Personal is Still Political', in Natasha Walter (ed.), op. cit., p26.

8 See Naomi Wolf, *Fire with Fire*, Chatto & Windus, London, 1993.

9 Ibid., p20.

10 Wendy Dennis, *Hot and Bothered: Sex and Love in the Nineties*, Viking Penguin, New York, 1992, p68. This is not a feminist critique but rather a guide to 'sexual etiquette' in the nineties, including questions such as 'Is there such a thing as a politically correct blowjob?'

11 Catharine Lumby, *Bad Girls: The Media, Sex and Feminism in the '90s*, Allen & Unwin, Sydney, 1997, pxxiv.

12 Virginia Woolf, *A Room of One's Own* (1929), Grafton Books, London, 1977, pp33-4.

13 The Spice Girls, *Girl Power!*, Zone/Chameleon Books, London, 1997, p15.

14 Myra Macdonald, op. cit., p220.

15 Cherry Norton, 'Stress Makes Working Women Lose Their Hair', *Sunday Times*, 2 November 1997, p1. Details of the study referred to reveal that 800 women were interviewed, throwing into sharp relief the article's claim that 'thousands of young women are losing their hair'.

16 Simone de Beauvoir, *The Second Sex* (1949), translated and edited by H.M. Parshley, Penguin Books, Harmondsworth, 1972, p295.

17 Germaine Greer, op. cit., p2.

18 Ibid., p3.

Chapter One

1 Susan Faludi, *Backlash: The Undeclared War Against Women*, Chatto & Windus, London, 1992, p2.

2 I have discussed this in '"A Doggy Fairy Tale": The Film Metamorphoses of *The Hundred and One Dalmatians*', in Deborah Cartmell and Imelda Whelehan (eds), *Adaptations: From Text to Screen, Screen to Text*, Routledge, London, 1999, pp214–225.

3 See Christine Hoff Sommers, *Who Stole Feminism?*, Touchstone Books, New York, 1994; Katie Roiphe, *The Morning After: Sex, Fear, and Feminism*, Hamish Hamilton, London, 1994; and Allan Bloom, *The Closing of the American Mind: How Higher Education has Failed Democracy and Impoverished the Soul of Today's Student*, Penguin, Harmondsworth, 1987.

4 See VéVé Clark, Shirley Nelson Garner, Margaret Higonnet and Ketu H. Katrak (eds), *Antifeminism in the Academy*, Routledge, New York, 1996.

5 Susan Faludi, op. cit., p16.

6 Ann Oakley, 'A Brief History of Gender', in Ann Oakley and Juliet Mitchell, *Who's Afraid of Feminism? Seeing Through the Backlash*, Hamish Hamilton, London, 1997, p33.

7 Germaine Greer, *The Whole Woman*, Doubleday, London, 1999, p153.

8 The example quoted was found in the *Guardian*, 8 March 1999, p10.
9 Natasha Walter, *The New Feminism*, Little, Brown and Company, London, 1998, p161.
10 Katie Roiphe, op. cit., p6.
11 Mary Ellmann, *Thinking About Women*, Virago, London, 1979, p29. Ellmann is specifically referring to the discussion of books by women, but I believe that the metaphor could be used more widely.
12 Richard Thomas, 'The Power of Women', *Observer*, 18 October 1998, p15.
13 Rene Denfeld, *The New Victorians: A Young Woman's Challenge to the Old Feminist Order*, Warner Books, New York, 1996, p16.
14 Ibid., p86.
15 See Imelda Whelehan, *Modern Feminist Thought: From the Second Wave to 'Post-feminism'*, Edinburgh University Press, Edinburgh, 1995, pp74–5.
16 Lynne Segal, *Straight Sex: The Politics of Pleasure*, Virago, London, 1994, pxi.
17 Shere Hite, *The Hite Report: A Nationwide Study of Female Sexuality*, Summit Books, London, 1977.
18 Included in Anne Koedt, Levine and A. Rapone (eds), *Radical Feminism*, Quadrangle Books, New York, 1973, but also reprinted in Sneja Gunew (ed.), *A Reader in Feminist Knowledge*, Routledge, London, 1991 and Stevi Jackson and Sue Scott (eds), *Feminism and Sexuality: A Reader*, Edinburgh University Press, Edinburgh, 1996.
19 Anna Coote and Beatrix Campbell, *Sweet Freedom: The Struggle for Women's Liberation* (second edn), Basil Blackwell, Oxford, 1987, p11.
20 Rene Denfeld, op. cit., p13.
21 Ibid., p19.
22 Ibid., p263.
23 Rosalind Coward, *Sacred Cows: Is Feminism Relevant to the New Millennium?*, HarperCollins, London, 1999, p3.
24 Ibid., p2.
25 Ibid., p71.
26 Ibid., p9.
27 Ibid., p50.

Chapter Two

1 See Sarah Younie, 'Girlie Culture: Popular Representations and Situating Discourses', unpublished conference paper. Special thanks to Sarah for giving me a copy of her work, and for several discussions on this and related topics.

2   Susan J. Douglas, *Where the Girls Are: Growing up Female with the Mass Media*, Time Books, New York, 1995, p97.
3   The Spice Girls, *Girl Power!*, Zone/Chameleon Books, London, 1997, p5.
4   Reported in the *Guardian*, 15 June 1999, p15.
5   See, for example, Caroline Sullivan, 'Saints Preserve Us', *Guardian* G2, 23 April 1999, pp14–15.
6   Mavis Bayton, *Frock Rock: Women Performing Popular Music*, Oxford University Press, Oxford, 1998, p65. Bayton's book is a fascinating account of women's experience in the popular music business, and picking out elements dealing with more high-profile women to fuel my own argument fails to do it justice.
7   Ibid., p75.
8   Ibid., p12.
9   Ibid., p13.
10   The Spice Girls, op. cit., p67.
11   Mavis Bayton, op. cit., p24.
12   Germaine Greer, *The Whole Woman*, Doubleday, London, 1999, p313.
13   Camille Paglia, 'Madonna 1: Animality and Artifice', in *Sex, Art and American Culture: Essays*, Penguin Books, Harmondsworth, 1993, p4.
14   The Spice Girls, op. cit., p48.
15   Jude Davies, '"It's Like Feminism, But You Don't Have to Burn Your Bra": Girl Power and the Spice Girls' breakthrough 1996–7', in Andrew Blake (ed.), *Living Through Pop*, Routledge, London, 1999, p162.
16   Joanna Burgin, 'Tell You What I Want!', in Jane Waghorn (ed.), *A Message for the Media: Young Women Talk*, The Women's Press, London, 1999, p92.
17   Jennifer Rickard, 'Loving and Hating the Spice Girls', in Jane Waghorn (ed.), op. cit., p36.
18   Quoted by Natasha Walter, *The New Feminism*, Little, Brown, London, 1998, p51.
19   See the Spice Girls, op. cit., pp16–17.
20   Phil Hilton, 'One of the Lads' in 'The Seven Deadly Sisters', *FHM*, September 1993, p67.
21   Alice Fisher, 'Babes with Brains?', *Everywoman*, April 1996, p22.
22   Quoted in Fisher, ibid., p23.
23   Cited in Veronica Lee, 'Meet the New Ladettes', *Guardian* G2, 17 January 1996, p13.
24   Cited in Decca Aitkenhead, 'Ooh, You Are Awful', *Guardian* G2, 25 August 1999, p4.
25   Or other kinds of personal adornment which because of age I suspect

have passed me by. With my 28 July to 10 August 1999 edition of *Mizz* I received free 'body jewels' accompanied by a picture of a disembodied young female midriff decorated with stencilling and featuring a 'body jewel' in the belly button.

26 Germaine Greer, op. cit., p319.

27 Ibid., p62.

28 This is cited unfavourably by Julie Burchill, who dubs the NCT the 'nipple police' in their quest to encourage more (especially working-class) women to breast-feed their babies. Burchill finds the campaign patronising and unfeminist: 'If a woman is happy to live as little more than a cow, she is free to do so. But she should not attempt to entrap her more modern sisters in her musty web.' In 'Breast-feeding? It Sucks!' *Guardian* G2, 12 May 1999, p9.

29 See Anita Chaudhuri, 'Doll Power', *Guardian* G2, 17 May 1999, pp6-7.

30 Mim from 21st Century Girls, interviewed in *Sugar*, September 1999, p83.

Chapter Three

1 Letters, *Loaded*, May 1997, p18.

2 *Loaded*, May 1997, p12.

3 Sean O'Hagan, 'The Re-invented Man', *Arena*, May–June 1991, p22.

4 Tim Edwards, *Men in the Mirror: Men's Fashion, Masculinity and Consumer Society*, Cassell, London, 1997, p82.

5 Sean Nixon, *Hard Looks: Masculinities, Spectatorship and Contemporary Consumption* UCL Press, London, 1996, p167.

6 Condé Nash press release, January 1991, quoted in Nixon, op. cit., p203.

7 Tim Edwards, op. cit., p78.

8 Katharine Viner, 'The Personal Is Still Political', in Natasha Walter (ed.), *On the Move: Feminism for a New Generation*, Virago, London, 1999, p13.

9 '15 Again', *Later*, May 1999, pp34–8.

10 Janice Doane and Devon Hodges, *Nostalgia and Sexual Difference: The Resistance to Contemporary Feminism*, Methuen, London, 1987, p3.

11 Cosmo Landesman, 'Boy Zone', *Guardian* G2, 1 December 1997, p9.

12 Ibid., p8.

13 Susan Faludi, *Stiffed: The Betrayal of the Modern Man*, Chatto & Windus, London, 1999, p527.

14 See Steve Busfield, 'Boy Thing Ads are "Not Sexist"', *Guardian*, 1 February 1999, p18.

15 Introduction to Robin Morgan (ed.), *Sisterhood is Powerful: An Anthology of Writings from the Women's Liberation Movement*, Vintage Books, New York, 1970, p1.

16 Cited in Duncan Campbell, 'Funny Business', *Guardian* G2, 23 August 1999, p4.
17 Though her participation in the show's finale, singing a duet with Skinner of the theme tune of the popular Australian soap *Home and Away*, was the most curious thing.
18 Ian Penman, 'Over Loaded', *Frank*, October 1997, p166.
19 Ibid., p169.
20 Ibid.
21 Suzanne Franks, *Having None of It: Women, Men and the Future of Work*, Granta Books, London, 1999, p167.
22 Julie Burchill, 'Way Back When Men Were Men', *Guardian* G2, 4 January 1999, p6.
23 Suzanne Franks, op. cit., p169.
24 Cited in Colin Blackstock, 'Many Men "View Rape as Acceptable"', *Guardian*, 25 September 1999, p8.
25 Dave Hill, *Men* (Predictions series), Phoenix, London, 1997, p37.
26 Ibid., p50.
27 Rosalind Coward, *Sacred Cows: Is Feminism Relevant to the New Millennium?*, HarperCollins, London, 1999, p10.

Chapter Four

1 Rosalind Coward, 'Women's War of Words', *Guardian*, 13 December 1997, p5.
2 Camille Paglia, 'Why British Sisters Suck', *Guardian*, 13 December 1997, p5.
3 This refers to the Seneca Falls Convention where the Declaration of Sentiments, a feminist appropriation of the Declaration of Independence, to call for suffrage and an end to prejudice, was drafted and signed.
4 Christine Hoff Sommers, *Who Stole Feminism?*, Touchstone Books, New York, 1994, p275.
5 Angela McRobbie, 'Pecs and Penises: The Meaning of Girlie Culture', *Soundings*, Issue 5, Spring 1997, pp160–61.
6 Special thanks to Lucy Powell for reminding me of the existence of this book.
7 Maureen Freely, *What About Us?: An Open Letter to the Mothers Feminism Forgot*, Bloomsbury Publishing, London, 1996, p1.
8 Ibid., p19.
9 Ibid., p47.
10 Ibid., p202.

11 Melissa Benn, *Madonna and Child: Towards a New Politics of Motherhood*, Jonathan Cape, London, 1998, p191.

12 Yvonne Roberts, *Mad About Women: Can There Ever be Fair Play Between the Sexes?*, Virago, London, 1992, p112.

13 Naomi Wolf, *Fire with Fire*, Chatto & Windus, London, 1993, p68.

14 Natasha Walter, 'Girls! New Feminism Needs You!', *New Statesman*, 16 January 1998, p18.

15 Natasha Walter, *The New Feminism*, Little, Brown and Company, London, 1998, p4.

16 Germaine Greer, *The Female Eunuch*, Paladin, London, 1971, p325.

17 Natasha Walter, op. cit., p175.

18 Ibid., pp221–53.

19 Rene Denfeld, *The New Victorians: A Young Woman's Challenge to the Old Feminist Order*, Warner Books, New York, 1996, pp266–79.

20 Printed in Michelene Wandor (ed.), *The Body Politic: Women's Liberation in Britain 1969–1972*, Stage 1, London, 1972, p2.

21 Melissa Benn, 'Contented, Complacent Women', *New Statesman*, 22 November 1996, p31.

22 Ibid.

23 Oona King, 'Why We Still Need Feminism', in Natasha Walter (ed.), *On the Move: Feminism for a New Generation*, Virago, London, 1999, p61.

24 Sophia Phoca, interviewed by Melaine Ashby, 'Beyond the New Feminism?', *Sibyl*, Issue 8, May–June 1999, p34.

25 Ann Brooks, *Postfeminisms: Feminism, Cultural Theory and Cultural Forms*, Routledge, London, 1997, p4.

26 Myra Macdonald, *Representing Women: Myths of Femininity in the Popular Media*, Edward Arnold, London, 1995, p100.

27 Michèle Roberts, 'Taking the P', *Guardian* G2, 11 October 1999.

28 Melissa Benn, op. cit., p21.

29 Angela McRobbie, *Postmodernism and Popular Culture*, Routledge, London, 1994, p73.

30 Germaine Greer, *The Whole Woman*, Doubleday, London, 1999, p6

31 Ibid., p43.

32 Ibid., p329.

33 Ibid., p309.

34 Ibid., p328.

35 Catherine Bennett, 'Greer: Kills All Known Germs', *Guardian* G2, 25 February 1999, p8.

36 Stella Tillyard, 'Germaine Greer', *Prospect*, April 1999, p48. Thanks to David Ryan for passing on this article.

37 Germaine Greer, op. cit., p1.
38 Ros Coward, 'Mad About the Girls', *Guardian* G2, 23 March 1998, p13.
39 Quoted in Maureen Freely, 'What Kate Did Next', *Observer Review*, 3 January 1999, p2.
40 'Girls! New Feminism Needs You!' *New Statesman*, 16 January 1998, p21.

Chapter Five

1   http://www.labour.org.uk
2   Kirsty Milne, 'Labour's Quota Women are on a Mission to Modernise', *New Statesman*, 16 May 1997, p17.
3   Ibid., p17.
4   As reported in *Towards Equality*, Autumn 1997, p3.
5   The website press release (downloaded in October 1999) makes no reference to whether future national selection processes will be changed. See http:/www.libdems.org.uk
6   Jane Pilcher, *Women in Contemporary Britain: An Introduction*, Routledge, London, 1999, p157.
7   Anne Perkins, 'So Far, So What?', *Guardian* G2, 29 April 1999, p6.
8   Ibid.
9   Actual figures are hard to come by, since figures depend upon MPs themselves specifying that they belong to a certain ethnic group. It seems that only two women, Diane Abbott and Oona King, have publicly identified themselves in this way. Thanks to the House of Commons Information Office for their help in this matter.
10 Helen Wilkinson, 'The Thatcher Legacy: Power Feminism and the Birth of Girl Power', in Natasha Walter (ed.), *On the Move: Feminism for a New Generation*, Virago, London, 1999, p39.
11 Ibid., p45.
12 See 'Women in the House of Commons', Factsheet No.5, http://www.parliament.uk/commons/lib (downloaded 15 June 1999).
13 Michèle Barrett, *Women's Oppression Today*, Verso, London, 1980, p207. Barrett's articulation of the family and its relation to women's oppression still remains one of the fullest.
14 Helen Wilkinson, 'The Day I Fell Out of Love with Blair', *New Statesman*, 7 August 1998, p9.
15 Suzanne Franks quotes one Labour 'insider' as saying, 'You knew for sure it was a New Lad administration when there were reminders to bring your football strip to the policy away days.' Suzanne Franks, *Having None of It: Women, Men and the Future of Work*, Granta Books, London, 1999, p38.

16 Quoted in Julia Hartley-Brewer, 'Maverick Fan Reaches her Goal', *Guardian,* 30 July 1999, p7.

17 Helen Wilkinson, op. cit., p10.

18 http://www.now.org/about.html (downloaded 13 August 1999).

19 Lucy Ward, 'Restructuring the Whole of Society. That's All We Want', *Guardian* G2, 1 June 1999, p7.

20 Harriet Harman, 'Sister Act', *Guardian* G2, 5 June 1997, p4.

21 Ibid.

22 Lucy Ward and Anne Perkins, 'New Role in Policy Making Across Whitehall', *Guardian,* 26 February 1998, p1.

23 Details from a speech by Ruddock given at the Fawcett Society AGM in June 1997 and reported in *Towards Equality* (Fawcett Society newsletter), Autumn 1997, p1.

24 Speech by Margaret Jay, Minister for Women, Bournemouth, 27 September 1999, reproduced on the Labour Party website at http:/www.labour.org.uk

25 Melissa Benn, 'The Reinvention of Harriet', *Guardian* G2, 29 June 1999, p6.

26 *Independent,* Wednesday Review, 3 March 1999, p1.

27 Melissa Benn, *Madonna and Child: Towards a New Politics of Motherhood,* Jonathan Cape, London, 1998, p168.

28 At the time of writing there are 121, as Jacqui Lait won a by-election in Beckenham after the 1997 General Election.

29 Cited in the *Guardian,* 17 June 1999, p12.

30 Libby Brooks, 'Some are More Equal than Others', *Guardian* G2, 11 November 1999, p3.

31 Reported in the *Guardian,* 22 May 1999, p22, and the *Daily Telegraph,* 19 May 1999, p16.

32 Susan Faludi, *Stiffed: The Betrayal of the Modern Man,* Chatto & Windus, London, p535.

33 Vivek Chaudhary, 'Woman Agent Challenges Footballers over Dinner Ban', *Guardian,* 3 August 1999, p6.

34 Reported in the *Guardian* (Linus Gregoriadis, 'Single Mother Wins Case over 16-hour Shifts'), 3 August 1999, p6.

35 Suzanne Franks, op. cit., p4.

36 Germaine Greer, *The Whole Woman,* Doubleday, London, 1999, p295.

Chapter Six

1 Lionel Tiger, *The Decline of Males,* Golden Books, New York, 1999.

2 Sheila Rowbotham, 'Women's Liberation and the New Politics', in

Michelene Wandor (ed.) *The Body Politic: Women's Liberation in Britain 1969–1972*, Stage 1, London, 1972, p3.

3 Suzanne Franks, *Having None of It: Women, Men and the Future of Work*, Granta Books, London, 1999, p12.

4 Ibid., p139.

5 Rosalind Coward, *Our Treacherous Hearts: Why Women Let Men Get Their Way*, Faber & Faber, London, 1992, p56.

6 Pete May, 'I'm Forever Blowing Bubbles Lulls Her to Sleep', *Guardian* G2, 16 June 1999, p7.

7 Ibid.

8 Julie Burchill, 'I Knew I Was Smart', *Guardian* Weekend, 4 April 1998, p7.

9 David Thomas, *Not Guilty: In Defence of Modern Man*, Weidenfeld & Nicolson, London, 1993, p7.

10 Ibid., p2.

11 'Have you any notion of how many books are written about women in the course of one year? Have you any notion how many are written by men? Are you aware that you are, perhaps, the most discussed animal in the universe?' Virginia Woolf, *A Room of One's Own* (1929), Grafton Books, London, 1977, p27.

12 See 'About the UKMM', http://www.ukmm.org.uk/about/content.htm (downloaded 6 August 1999).

13 Suzanne Franks, op cit., pp148–50.

14 http://www.ukmm.org.uk/camp/eoc.htm (downloaded 17 November 1999).

15 David Thomas, op cit., p8.

16 Ibid., p12.

17 Richard Collier, 'The New Man: Fact or Fad?', originally collected in *Achilles Heel*, Issue 14, Winter 1992/1993; downloaded from http://www.stejonda.demon.co.uk/achilles on 6 August 1999.

18 'Promise Keepers' website: http//:www.promisekeepers.org, downloaded on 6 August 1999.

19 See http://www.now.org/issues/right/promise/mythfact.html (downloaded 6 August 1999).

20 Cited in Andrew Pulver, 'Fight the Good Fight', *Guardian* G2, 29 October 1999, p2.

21 Mariah Burton Nelson, *The Stronger Women Get, the More Men Love Football: Sexism and the Culture of Sport*, The Women's Press, London, 1996, p7.

22 Ibid., p118.

23 Rosalind Coward, *Sacred Cows: Is Feminism Relevant to the New Millennium?*, HarperCollins, 1999, p44.

24 Ibid., p90.

25 Ibid., p93.

26 Nick Hornby, *Fever Pitch*, Victor Gollancz, London, 1992, p11. Thanks to Mark Sandle for the loan of his copy.

27 Susan Faludi, *Stiffed: The Betrayal of the Modern Man*, Chatto & Windus, London, 1999, p528.

28 Ibid., p599.

Chapter Seven

1 Aminatta Forna, 'Sellout', in Natasha Walter (ed.), *On the Move: Feminism for a New Generation*, Virago, London, 1999, p140.

2 Helen Fielding, *Bridget Jones's Diary*, Picador, London, 1996, p20.

3 Ibid., p59.

4 Helen Gurley Brown, *Sex and the Single Girl*, Bernard Geis Associates, New York, 1962, p3.

5 Ibid., p4.

6 Ibid., p11.

7 Ibid., p10.

8 Ibid., p70.

9 Carol Sarler, 'Cosmo's Climax Control', *Sunday Times* Magazine, 28 February 1993, p21.

10 Susan J. Douglas, *Where the Girls Are: Growing up Female with the Mass Media*, Time Books, New York, 1995, p69.

11 Published by the Social Affairs Unit, 1997.

12 Linda Grant, 'Meanwhile, Back in the Real World', *Guardian*, 25 November 1997, p8.

13 See Janice Radway, *Reading the Romance: Women, Patriarchy and Popular Culture*, Verso, London, 1987.

14 Mariah Burton Nelson sees these ads in a more favourable light than I do, pointing out that they are part of a consciously woman-centred approach which has won them acclaim and even a feature on the Oprah Winfrey Show, as well as, needless to say, boosted sales. See *The Stronger Women Get, the More Men Love Football: Sexism and the Culture of Sport*, The Women's Press, London, 1996, pp223–4.

15 'The Big Sleaze', *Elle*, February 1994.

16 *Company*, April 1996.

17 *Elle*, March 1996.

18 Ibid.

19 Reported in the *Guardian* G2, 27 July 1999, p7 (Victoria Coren, 'Next Year's Models').

20 See Libby Brooks, 'Crown of Thorns', *Guardian* G2, 26 May 1999, p5.
21 Ibid.
22 Yvonne Roberts, 'Mum's not the Word', *Guardian* G2, 15 April 1999, p5.
23 See Susie Orbach, *Guardian* G2, 10 February 1998, p4.
24 Germaine Greer, *The Whole Woman*, Doubleday, London 1999, p23.
25 Naomi Wolf, *The Beauty Myth*, Chatto & Windus, London, 1990, p65.
26 Naomi Wolf, *Fire with Fire*, Chatto & Windus, London, 1993, p323.
27 Ros Ballaster, Margaret Beetham, Elizabeth Frazer and Sandra Hebron, *Women's Worlds: Ideology, Femininity and the Woman's Magazine*, Macmillan, London, 1991, p174.
28 Reported in the *Guardian* G2, 30 March 1999, p7.
29 Imelda Whelehan and Esther Sonnet, '"Freedom From" or "Freedom To"…? Contemporary Identities in Women's Magazines', in Mary Maynard and June Purvis (eds), *(Hetero)sexual Politics*, Taylor & Francis, London, 1995, p83.
30 Helen Fielding, *Bridget Jones's Diary*, Picador, London, 1996, pp126–7.
31 Paul Wallace, *Agequake: Riding the Demographic Rollercoaster Shaking Business, Finance and Our World*, Nicholas Brealey Publishing, London, 1999, p13.
32 Ibid., p14.

Chapter Eight

1 Susan J Douglas, *Where the Girls Are: Growing Up Female With the Mass Media*, Time Books, New York, 1994, p215.
2 bell hooks, *Ain't I a Woman: Black Women and Feminism*, Pluto Press, London, 1982, p32.
3 Patricia Hill Collins, *Black Feminist Thought: Knowledge Consciousness, and the Politics of Empowerment*, Routledge, New York, 1991, p79.
4 Annecka Marshall, 'From Sexual Denigration to Self-respect', in Delia Jarrett-Macauley (ed.), *Reconstructing Womanhood, Reconstructing Feminism: Writings on Black Women*, Routledge, London, 1996, p33.
5 Jenny McLeod, 'Still Rising', in Natasha Walter (ed.), *On the Move: Feminism for a New Generation*, Virago, London, 1999, p122.
6 Ibid., p133.
7 Helen Kolawole, 'Who You Calling a Bitch?', *Everywoman*, March 1996, pp22–3.
8 Ibid., p23.
9 Stephanie Theobald, 'Lesbians on Horseback', in Natasha Walter (ed.), op. cit., p93.
10 Cherry Smyth, 'Playing it Straight', *Everywoman*, April 1994, p18.

11 Alexander Doty and Ben Gove, 'Queer Representation in the Mass Media', in Andy Medhurst and Sally R. Munt (eds), *Lesbian and Gay Studies*, Cassell, London, 1997, p86.
12 See Joan Nestle, *A Restricted Country: Essays and Short Stories*, Sheba Feminist Publishers, London, 1987.
13 Precious Williams, 'Notting Hill: The Place, Not the Film', *Pride*, August 1999, p18.
14 Ibid., p20.

Chapter Nine

1 Paul Wallace, *Agequake: Riding the Demographic Rollercoaster Shaking Business, Finance and our World*, Nicholas Brealey Publishing, London, 1999, p214.
2 Francis Fukuyama, *The Great Disruption: Human Nature and the Reconstitution of Social Order*, Profile Books, London, 1999, p121.
3 Ibid., p98.
4 Charlotte Raven, 'Have British Feminists Given Up the Fight?', *Guardian* G2, 27 July 1999, p5.
5 Rosalind Coward, *Sacred Cows: Is Feminism Relevant to the New Millennium?*, HarperCollins, London, 1999, p16.
6 Susan J. Douglas, *Where the Girls Are: Growing Up Female with the Mass Media*, Times Books, New York, 1995, p5.

Index